Reynolds

Incredibly Easy

Cooking with FOIL AND MORE

pil

Publications International, Ltd.

Pictured on the front cover: Baby Back Barbecued Ribs *(page 34).*

Pictured on the back cover: Herbed Vegetable Packets *(page 44).*

ISBN-13: 978-1-4127-2663-4
ISBN-10: 1-4127-2663-8

Manufactured in China.

8 7 6 5 4 3 2 1

Microwave Cooking: Microwave ovens vary in wattage. Use the cooking times as guidelines
and check for doneness before adding more time.

Preparation/Cooking Times: Preparation times are based on the approximate amount of
time required to assemble the recipe before cooking, baking, chilling, or serving. These times
include preparation steps such as measuring, chopping, and mixing. The fact that some
preparations and cooking can be done simultaneously is taken into account. Preparation of
optional ingredients and serving suggestions is not included.

Contents

Easy Recipes from the Reynolds Kitchens

Reynolds Incredibly Easy Cooking with Foil & More has recipes specially designed for today's busy cook. Brought to you from the Reynolds Kitchens, these recipes, tips and timesavers were developed to help streamline your mealtime prep and cleanup. The majority of the Incredibly Easy Foil recipes feature Reynolds Wrap® Foil, America's favorite aluminum foil. Reynolds Wrap Foil is tough enough to stand up to your most challenging cooking and grilling tasks. It's versatile too. You can roast, grill, bake, cover, freeze and store your most demanding recipes with confidence. When you use Reynolds Wrap Foil your meals will come out just how you intended: delicious with mess-free cleanup.

No Soaking! No Scrubbing! No Kidding!

Line pans with Reynolds Wrap® Heavy Duty Aluminum Foil before you cook to avoid scrubbing afterwards.

1. TURN pan upside down and press a sheet of foil around it.

2. REMOVE foil, flip pan over and drop foil inside.

3. CRIMP the edges and you're ready to cook!

When using Release® Non-Stick Foil, follow the above directions, making sure that the non-stick (dull) side is facing down toward the pan when pressing foil around the pan. The non-stick side of the foil liner will be facing up toward the food when dropped inside the pan.

Reynolds Quick & Easy Packet Cooking

A simple, no-mess way to make delicious homecooked meals.

When you wrap food in Reynolds Wrap® Heavy Duty Aluminum Foil packets and then oven bake or grill it, the ingredients cook evenly and quickly, and there's no cleanup! Packet cooking also lets you customize your meals to suit the individual tastes in your family—if someone doesn't like an ingredient, such as pepper or onions, just leave that ingredient out of their foil packet. And for the family eating at different times, make up individual meals in foil packets and refrigerate. Packets can be baked in the oven one at a time or up to four at once as family schedules permit.

1. **CENTER** ingredients on a sheet (12×18 inches) of Reynolds Wrap® Heavy Duty Aluminum Foil.

2. **BRING** up foil sides. Double fold top and ends to seal packet, leaving room for heat circulation inside. Repeat to make four packets.

3. **BAKE** on a cookie sheet in preheated 450°F oven **OR GRILL** on medium-high in covered grill.

4. **AFTER COOKING,** open end of foil packet first to allow steam to escape. Then open top of foil packet.

Slow Cooker Chicken Fajitas

Mexican Chicken Dinner Packets for Two

Baked Fiesta Enchiladas

Basil Chicken Packets

Easy Weeknight
Meals

Ginger Chicken Packets

Prep Time: 10 minutes ■ Cook Time: 18 minutes

- **4 sheets (12×18 inches *each*) Reynolds Wrap® Heavy Duty Aluminum Foil**
- **⅓ cup light teriyaki sauce**
- **1 tablespoon sesame oil**
- **1 teaspoon grated fresh ginger**
- **4 boneless, skinless chicken breast halves (1 to 1¼ pounds)**
- **2 cups broccoli florets**
- **1 medium red bell pepper, cut into ½-inch strips**
- **¼ pound fresh mushrooms, quartered**
- **Hot cooked rice (optional)**

PREHEAT oven to 450°F **OR** grill to medium-high. Combine teriyaki sauce, sesame oil and ginger; set aside.

CENTER one chicken breast half on *each* sheet of Reynolds Wrap Heavy Duty Aluminum Foil. Top with vegetables.

BRING up foil sides. Double fold top and one end of packet. Through open end, add one-fourth of teriyaki mixture. Double fold remaining end to seal packet, leaving room for heat circulation inside. Repeat to make four packets.

BAKE 18 to 22 minutes on a cookie sheet in oven **OR GRILL** 13 to 15 minutes in covered grill. Serve over rice, if desired.

Makes 4 servings

Tamale Chicken Packets

Prep Time: 10 minutes ■ Cook Time: 15 minutes

**4 sheets (12×18 inches *each*) Reynolds Wrap® Release®
  Non-Stick Foil**
1 can (15¼ ounces) whole kernel corn, drained
¼ cup chopped green bell pepper
¼ cup sliced ripe olives
2 cups coarsely crushed tortilla chips
1 cup chunky salsa, divided
**4 boneless, skinless chicken breast halves (1 to 1¼ pounds), cut
  into ½-inch strips**
1 teaspoon *each* onion salt and chili powder
1 cup shredded Cheddar cheese

PREHEAT oven to 450°F **OR** grill to medium-high.

CENTER one-fourth of corn on *each* sheet of Reynolds Wrap Release Non-Stick
Foil. Top with green pepper, olives, tortilla chips and half of salsa. Add chicken;
sprinkle with onion salt and chili powder. Top with remaining salsa.

BRING up foil sides. Double fold top and ends to seal packet, leaving room for
heat circulation inside. Repeat to make four packets.

BAKE 15 to 18 minutes on a cookie sheet in oven **OR GRILL** 12 to 14 minutes
in covered grill. Sprinkle with cheese before serving. Serve with additional salsa
and crushed chips, if desired.

Makes 4 servings

Slow Cooker Pot Roast

Prep Time: 15 minutes ■ Cook Time: 8 hours

1 **Reynolds® Slow Cooker Liner**
¼ **cup water**
4 **medium red potatoes, cut into quarters**
1 **medium onion, cut into quarters**
1 **package (16 ounces) peeled baby carrots**
1 **envelope (1 ounce) onion soup mix, divided**
¼ **teaspoon *each* salt, black pepper and dried thyme**
1 **(2½- to 3-pound) boneless beef chuck pot roast**

OPEN Reynolds Slow Cooker Liner and place it inside a 5- to 6½-quart slow cooker bowl. Fit liner snugly against the bottom and sides of bowl; pull top of liner over rim of bowl.

PLACE water and three-fourths of the vegetables in slow cooker liner. Reserve 1 tablespoon onion soup mix. Sprinkle remaining onion soup mix over vegetables; stir gently to coat evenly. Sprinkle and rub salt, pepper and thyme over the pot roast. Place pot roast on top of vegetables. Place remaining vegetables around pot roast; sprinkle with remaining onion soup mix. Place lid on slow cooker.

COOK on LOW for 8 to 9 hours **OR** on HIGH for 5 to 6 hours or until pot roast is tender.

CAREFULLY remove lid to allow steam to escape. Serve food directly from slow cooker. Do not lift or transport liner with food inside. Cool slow cooker completely; remove liner and toss.

Makes 6 to 8 (3-ounce) servings

**REYNOLDS
KITCHENS TIP:**

Substitute four peeled white potatoes for red potatoes. Substitute four whole carrots, peeled, cut into two-inch pieces for baby carrots.

Slow Cooker Chicken Fajitas

Prep Time: 10 minutes ■ Cook Time: 6 hours

- 1 **Reynolds® Slow Cooker Liner**
- 2 **pounds boneless, skinless chicken breast halves**
- 1 **medium onion, thinly sliced**
- 1 **large red bell pepper, cut into thin strips**
- 1 **large green bell pepper, cut into thin strips**
- ¾ **cup chunky salsa**
- 2 **packages (1.4 ounces *each*) fajita seasoning mix**
- ¼ **teaspoon cayenne pepper**
- 16 **10-inch flour tortillas**
  Shredded cheese, chopped tomatoes, guacamole, sour cream (optional)

OPEN Reynolds Slow Cooker Liner and place it inside a 5- to 6½-quart slow cooker bowl. Fit liner snugly against the bottom and sides of bowl; pull top of liner over rim of bowl.

PLACE chicken in slow cooker liner. Place onions and bell peppers on top of chicken.

MIX salsa, fajita seasoning mix and cayenne pepper in a medium bowl. Pour over chicken. Place lid on slow cooker.

COOK on LOW for 6 to 7 hours **OR** on HIGH for 3 to 4 hours or until chicken is done.

CAREFULLY remove lid to allow steam to escape. Gently stir chicken and sauce with a plastic or wooden slotted spoon to break chicken into strips. Spoon ½ cup chicken mixture into center of *each* tortilla; add desired toppings. Fold tortilla over filling. Do not lift or transport liner with food inside. Cool slow cooker completely; remove liner and toss.

Makes 8 servings

Super Italian Meatballs

Prep Time: 15 minutes   ■   Cook Time: 30 minutes

- 1 **Reynolds® Oven Bag, Large Size**
- 1 **tablespoon all-purpose flour**
- 1 **jar (about 26 ounces) pasta sauce, divided**
- 1 **pound ground beef**
- ½ **small red bell pepper, finely chopped**
- ¼ **cup bread crumbs**
- 1 **egg**
- 1½ **teaspoons dried Italian seasoning**
- 1 **teaspoon *each* salt and garlic powder**
   Hot cooked pasta or hoagie rolls
   Shredded Parmesan cheese (optional)

PREHEAT oven to 350°F.

SHAKE flour in Reynolds Oven Bag; place bag in 13×9×2-inch or larger baking pan at least 2 inches deep. Pour ⅔ cup pasta sauce in a large bowl; set aside. Add remaining pasta sauce to bag; squeeze bag to blend in flour.

ADD ground beef, bell peppers, bread crumbs, egg and spices to pasta sauce in bowl; mix until well blended. Use about ⅓ cup mixture to form *each* meatball. Place meatballs in an even layer in oven bag.

CLOSE oven bag with nylon tie; cut six ½-inch slits in top. Tuck ends of bag in pan.

BAKE 30 to 35 minutes or until meat thermometer inserted into meatballs reads 160°F. Serve meatballs and sauce over hot cooked pasta **OR** cut meatballs in half and serve on hoagie rolls as meatball subs. Sprinkle shredded Parmesan cheese over meatballs, if desired.

Makes 8 to 9 large meatballs

REYNOLDS KITCHENS TIP:

Use lean or super lean ground beef if you like, because Reynolds Oven Bags hold in the natural juices to make meatballs flavorful and juicy without the additional fat.

Easy Pork Chop Packets

Prep Time: 10 minutes ■ Cook Time: 16 minutes

- 4 **sheets (12×18 inches *each*) Reynolds Wrap® Heavy Duty Aluminum Foil**
- 1 **small onion, thinly sliced**
- 4 **boneless pork chops, about ½-inch thick**
  Salt and black pepper to taste
- 1 **can (10¾ ounces) cream of mushroom soup, undiluted**
- 2 **tablespoons soy sauce**
- 1 **medium green bell pepper, sliced**
  Hot cooked rice

PREHEAT oven to 450°F **OR** grill to medium-high.

CENTER onion slices on *each* sheet of Reynolds Wrap Heavy Duty Aluminum Foil. Top with pork chops; sprinkle with salt and pepper. Combine cream of mushroom soup and soy sauce; spoon over pork chops. Top with green pepper slices.

BRING up foil sides. Double fold top and ends to seal packet, leaving room for heat circulation inside. Repeat to make four packets.

BAKE 16 to 18 minutes on a cookie sheet in oven **OR GRILL** 10 to 12 minutes in covered grill. Serve over rice.

Makes 4 servings

Tex Mex Meat Loaf Packets

Prep Time: 10 minutes   ■   Cook Time: 18 minutes

- **4 sheets (12×18 inches *each*) Reynolds Wrap® Release® Non-Stick Foil**
- **1 pound extra lean ground beef**
- **¼ cup finely crushed tortilla chips**
- **¼ cup finely chopped onion**
- **2 teaspoons chili powder**
- **2 teaspoons Worcestershire sauce**
- **½ teaspoon garlic salt**
- **¾ cup barbecue sauce, divided**
- **1 package (10 ounces) frozen whole kernel corn OR 1 can (15¼ ounces) whole kernel corn, drained**

PREHEAT oven to 450°F **OR** grill to medium-high. Combine lean ground beef, tortilla chips, onion, chili powder, Worcestershire sauce, garlic salt and ¼ cup barbecue sauce. Shape mixture into four meat loaves, flattening slightly.

CENTER one meat loaf on *each* sheet of Reynolds Wrap Release Non-Stick Foil with nonstick (dull) side toward food. Top with corn. Spoon remaining barbecue sauce over meat loaf and corn.

BRING up foil sides. Double fold top and ends to seal packet, leaving room for heat circulation inside. Repeat to make four packets.

BAKE 18 to 20 minutes on a cookie sheet in oven **OR GRILL** 12 to 14 minutes in covered grill.

Makes 4 servings

Slow Cooker Herbed Chicken

Prep Time: 10 minutes ■ Cook Time: 5 hours

1 **Reynolds® Slow Cooker Liner**
1 **(3- to 4-pound) whole chicken**
1 **teaspoon** *each* **dried basil and seasoned salt**
½ **teaspoon** *each* **black pepper and garlic powder**
2 **tablespoons fresh lemon juice**
1 **tablespoon butter, melted**

OPEN Reynolds Slow Cooker Liner and place it inside a 5- to 6½-quart slow cooker bowl. Fit liner snugly against the bottom and sides of bowl; pull top of liner over rim of bowl.

PLACE chicken in slow cooker liner. Mix spices; sprinkle 1 teaspoon mixture into chicken cavity. Sprinkle remaining seasonings over chicken. Drizzle with lemon juice and butter. Place lid on slow cooker.

COOK on LOW for 5 to 6 hours **OR** on HIGH for 3 to 4 hours or until meat thermometer inserted into thickest part of chicken thigh not touching bone reads 180°F.

CAREFULLY remove lid to allow steam to escape. Place chicken on a platter to slice and serve. Do not lift or transport liner with food inside. Cool slow cooker completely; remove liner and toss.

Makes 5 to 6 servings

REYNOLDS KITCHENS TIPS:

- *To reduce fat and calories, remove skin from chicken before eating.*
- *Substitute olive oil for melted butter, if desired.*

Mexican Chicken Dinner Packets for Two

Prep Time: 5 minutes ■ Cook Time: 15 minutes

- **2 sheets (12×18 inches *each*) Reynolds Wrap® Release® Non-Stick Foil**
- **2 boneless, skinless chicken breast halves (½ to ¾ pound)**
- **½ cup chunky salsa**
- **⅔ cup black beans or kidney beans (from 15-ounce can), drained**
- **½ cup shredded Mexican blend or Cheddar cheese**
  Tortilla chips (optional)

PREHEAT oven to 450°F **OR** grill to medium-high.

CENTER one chicken breast half on *each* sheet of Reynolds Wrap Release Non-Stick Foil with non-stick (dull) side toward food. Spoon salsa over chicken; top with beans.

BRING up foil sides. Double fold top and ends to seal packet, leaving room for heat circulation inside. Repeat to make two packets.

BAKE 15 to 18 minutes on a cookie sheet in oven **OR GRILL** 11 to 13 minutes in covered grill; sprinkle with cheese before serving. Serve with tortilla chips, if desired.

Makes 2 servings

Shrimp en Papillote with Pasta

Prep Time: 15 minutes ■ Cook Time: 13 minutes

Reynolds® Parchment Paper

1 **pound medium raw shrimp, peeled and deveined**
¼ **cup olive oil**
2 **tablespoons chopped fresh parsley**
2 **to 4 cloves garlic, minced**
⅛ **teaspoon** *each* **seasoned salt and black pepper**
8 **fresh lemon slices**

PASTA

½ **package (1 pound) angel hair pasta, cooked**
¼ **cup grated Parmesan cheese**
¼ **cup oil-packed sun-dried tomatoes, drained**
2 **tablespoons olive oil**
1 **tablespoon chopped fresh parsley**

PREHEAT oven to 400°F.

TEAR off four 15-inch sheets of Reynolds Parchment Paper. Fold *each* parchment sheet in half.

UNFOLD *each* parchment sheet. Place one-fourth of shrimp on *each* sheet near fold. Mix olive oil, parsley, garlic, seasoned salt and pepper in a small bowl. Drizzle one-fourth of olive oil mixture over shrimp and top with two lemon slices.

FOLD over other half of *each* parchment sheet to enclose ingredients. To seal edges together, start at the top corner, making small overlapping folds down entire length of packet. At the end of the packet, twist the last fold several times to make a tight seal. Repeat to make 4 packets. Place parchment packets on a large cookie sheet.

BAKE 13 to 15 minutes. While packets are baking, toss hot pasta with Parmesan cheese, sun-dried tomatoes, olive oil and parsley. Place cooked parchment packets on one side of dinner plate. Carefully cut an "X" in top of *each* packet to allow steam to escape. Serve immediately with pasta on other half of plate.

Makes 4 servings

Pesto Snapper en Papillote

Prep Time: 15 minutes   ■   Cook Time: 15 minutes

Reynolds® Parchment Paper
4   red snapper fillets (4 to 6 ounces *each*)
4   teaspoons basil pesto
1   cup grape tomatoes, halved
½   of a yellow bell pepper, cut into rings

PREHEAT oven to 400°F. Tear off four 15-inch sheets of Reynolds Parchment Paper. Fold each sheet in half and crease it in the center. Unfold.

PLACE one snapper fillet on one-half of *each* sheet near crease. Spread 1 teaspoon pesto onto *each* snapper fillet. Top *each* fillet with tomatoes and bell pepper rings.

FOLD over other half of sheet to enclose ingredients. Starting at top corner, make small overlapping folds down entire length of packet to seal edges together. Twist the last fold several times to make a tight seal. Repeat to make four packets. Place parchment packets on a large cookie sheet.

BAKE 15 to 17 minutes. Place parchment packets on dinner plates. Carefully cut an "✕" in top of *each* packet to allow steam to escape. Serve immediately.

Makes 4 servings

No Fuss Chicken & Green Bean Dinner

Prep Time: 15 minutes ■ Cook Time: 45 minutes

- 1 **Reynolds® Oven Bag, Large Size**
- 1 **tablespoon flour**
- 1 **can (10¾ ounces) cream of mushroom soup**
- 1 **package (9 ounces) frozen cut green beans, thawed**
- ½ **cup chicken broth or water**
- ¼ **teaspoon pepper**
- 1 **can (2.8 ounces) French fried onions, divided**
- 6 **skinless chicken pieces**
  Seasoned salt and black pepper to taste

PREHEAT oven to 350°F.

SHAKE flour in Reynolds Oven Bag; place in 13×9×2-inch or larger baking pan at least 2 inches deep.

ADD soup, green beans, chicken broth, pepper and ½ can onions to oven bag. Squeeze oven bag to blend in flour. Arrange ingredients in an even layer in oven bag. Sprinkle chicken with seasoned salt and pepper. Place chicken in oven bag on top of soup mixture. Sprinkle remaining onions on top of chicken. Tuck ends of bag in pan.

CLOSE oven bag with nylon tie; cut six ½-inch slits in top.

BAKE 45 to 50 minutes or until chicken is tender. Stir sauce before serving.

Makes 4 to 6 servings

Chicken Divan Packets

Prep Time: 10 minutes ■ Cook Time: 20 minutes

- **4 sheets (12×18 inches *each*) Reynolds Wrap® Heavy Duty Aluminum Foil**
- **4 boneless, skinless chicken breast halves (1 to 1¼ pounds)**
- **3 cups frozen broccoli florets**
- **1 can (10¾ ounces) cream of chicken and broccoli soup, undiluted**
- **1½ cups sliced fresh mushrooms**
- **1 cup shredded Cheddar cheese**
- **Hot cooked rice**

PREHEAT oven to 450°F **OR** grill to medium-high.

CENTER one chicken breast half on *each* sheet of Reynolds Wrap Heavy Duty Aluminum Foil. Arrange broccoli around chicken. Combine soup, mushrooms and cheese; spoon sauce over chicken and broccoli.

BRING up foil sides. Double fold top and ends to seal packet, leaving room for heat circulation inside. Repeat to make four packets.

BAKE 20 to 24 minutes on a cookie sheet in oven **OR GRILL** 16 to 18 minutes in covered grill. Serve over rice.

Makes 4 servings

REYNOLDS KITCHENS TIP:

Substitute reduced-fat soup.

Lemon Rosemary Chicken en Papillote

Prep Time: 15 minutes ■ Cook Time: 20 minutes

Reynolds® Parchment Paper
- 1 **tablespoon grated lemon peel**
- 1 **tablespoon olive oil**
- ½ **teaspoon crushed dried rosemary**
- ½ **teaspoon seasoned salt**
- ½ **teaspoon coarsely ground black pepper**
- 4 **boneless, skinless chicken breast halves (1 to 1¼ pounds)**
- 1 **package (8 ounces) sugar snap peas**
- 1 **medium yellow squash, sliced**
- ½ **cup roasted red pepper, thinly sliced**

PREHEAT oven to 400°F. Tear off four 15-inch sheets of Reynolds Parchment Paper. Fold each sheet in half and crease it in the center. Unfold.

MIX lemon peel, olive oil, rosemary, seasoned salt and pepper in a small bowl until well blended; set aside. Place one chicken breast on one-half of *each* sheet near crease. Spread about ½ teaspoon seasoning mixture over *each* chicken breast. Place peas, squash and red pepper around chicken.

FOLD over other half of sheet to enclose ingredients. Starting at top corner, make small overlapping folds down entire length of packet to seal edges together. Twist the last fold several times to make a tight seal. Repeat to make 4 packets. Place parchment packets on a large cookie sheet.

BAKE 20 to 25 minutes. Place parchment packets on dinner plates. Carefully cut an "✕" in top of *each* packet to allow steam to escape. Serve immediately.

Makes 4 servings

Barbecue Chicken Packets

Prep Time: 8 minutes ■ Cook Time: 18 minutes

4   **sheets (12×18 inches *each*) Reynolds Wrap® Heavy Duty Aluminum Foil**
4   **boneless, skinless chicken breast halves (1 to 1¼ pounds)**
1   **cup barbecue sauce**
1   **can (15¼ ounces) whole kernel corn, drained**
½   **cup chopped green bell pepper**

PREHEAT oven to 450°F **OR** grill to medium-high.

CENTER one chicken breast half on *each* sheet of Reynolds Wrap Heavy Duty Aluminum Foil. Spoon barbecue sauce over chicken. Top with vegetables.

BRING up foil sides. Double fold top and ends to seal packet, leaving room for heat circulation inside. Repeat to make four packets.

BAKE 18 to 22 minutes on a cookie sheet in oven **OR GRILL** 12 to 15 minutes in covered grill.

Makes 4 servings

Salmon en Papillote

Prep Time: 20 minutes ■ Cook Time: 18 minutes

Reynolds® Parchment Paper
2 **tablespoons olive oil**
1 **teaspoon dried tarragon leaves**
2 **cloves garlic, minced**
1 **teaspoon grated lemon peel**
½ **teaspoon seasoned salt**
¼ **teaspoon black pepper**
1 **pound fresh asparagus**
4 **salmon fillets (4 to 6 ounces *each*), skin removed**
4 **lemon slices**

PREHEAT oven to 400°F. Tear off four 15-inch sheets of Reynolds Parchment Paper. Fold each sheet in half and crease it in the center. Unfold.

MIX olive oil, tarragon, garlic, lemon peel, seasoned salt and pepper in a small bowl; set aside. Place one-fourth of asparagus evenly on one-half of *each* sheet near crease. Place salmon fillet on top of asparagus. Spread *each* fillet with one-fourth of olive oil mixture. Top *each* fillet with a lemon slice.

FOLD over other half of sheet to enclose ingredients. Starting at top corner, make small overlapping folds down entire length of packet to seal edges together. Twist the last fold several times to make a tight seal. Repeat to make four packets. Place parchment packets on a large cookie sheet.

BAKE 18 to 20 minutes. Place parchment packets on dinner plates. Carefully cut an "✕" in top of *each* packet to allow steam to escape. Serve immediately.

Makes 4 servings

Asian-Style Pork Tenderloin

Prep Time: 15 minutes ■ Cook Time: 45 minutes

- 1 **Reynolds® Oven Bag, Large Size**
- 2 **pork tenderloins (about 1½ pounds *each*)**
- ¾ **cup salsa**
- ¼ **cup honey roasted-flavor peanut butter**
- 2 **tablespoons all-purpose flour**
- 2 **tablespoons *each* soy sauce and sesame oil**
- 1 **teaspoon grated fresh ginger**
- ¼ to ½ **teaspoon cayenne pepper**
- 3 **cloves garlic, minced**
  Hot cooked rice
- ¼ **cup coarsely chopped peanuts or cashews**
- 2 **tablespoons chopped green onion**

PREHEAT oven to 350°F. Place Reynolds Oven Bag in 13×9×2-inch or larger baking pan at least two inches deep.

PLACE pork in oven bag. Mix salsa, peanut butter, flour, soy sauce, sesame oil, ginger, cayenne pepper and garlic in a medium bowl. Stir until smooth; spoon over pork.

CLOSE oven bag with nylon tie; cut six ½-inch slits in top. Tuck ends of bag in pan.

BAKE 45 to 50 minutes or until meat thermometer reads 160°F. Spoon rice onto serving platter. Place pork on top of rice. Stir sauce; spoon over pork. Sprinkle with peanuts and green onion.

Makes 10 to 12 servings

Basil Chicken Packets

Prep Time: 12 minutes ■ Cook Time: 16 minutes

- **4 sheets (12×18 inches *each*) Reynolds Wrap® Heavy Duty Aluminum Foil**
- **4 boneless, skinless chicken breast halves (1 to 1¼ pounds)**
- **2 tablespoons chopped fresh parsley**
- **2 to 3 teaspoons grated lemon peel**
- **1½ teaspoons dried basil**
- **½ teaspoon salt**
- **2 medium yellow squash, sliced**
- **1 medium red bell pepper, cut into rings**
- **Freshly ground black pepper to taste**

PREHEAT oven to 450°F **OR** grill to medium-high.

CENTER one chicken breast half on *each* sheet of Reynolds Wrap Heavy Duty Aluminum Foil. Combine parsley, lemon peel, basil and salt; sprinkle over chicken. Top with squash and bell pepper. Sprinkle with black pepper

BRING up foil sides. Double fold top and ends to seal packet, leaving room for heat circulation inside. Repeat to make four packets.

BAKE 16 to 18 minutes on a cookie sheet in oven **OR GRILL** 11 to 13 minutes in covered grill.

Makes 4 servings

Baby Back Barbecue Ribs

Prep Time: 5 minutes ▨ Grill Time: 1 hour

 2 **sheets (18x24 inches *each*) Reynolds Wrap® Heavy Duty Aluminum Foil**
 3 **pounds baby back pork ribs**
 1 **tablespoon packed brown sugar**
 1 **tablespoon paprika**
 2 **teaspoons garlic powder**
1½ **teaspoons black pepper**
 ½ **cup water OR 6 to 8 ice cubes, divided**
1½ **cups barbecue sauce**
    Reynolds Wrap® Release® Non-Stick Foil

PREHEAT grill to medium.

CENTER half of ribs in a single layer on each sheet of Reynolds Wrap Heavy Duty Aluminum Foil. Combine brown sugar and spices in a small bowl; rub over ribs, turning to coat evenly.

BRING up foil sides. Double fold top and one end to seal packet. Through open end, add ¼ cup water or 3 to 4 ice cubes. Double fold remaining end, leaving room for heat circulation inside. Repeat to make two packets.

GRILL 45 to 60 minutes in covered grill. Remove ribs from foil packet. Make drainage holes in a sheet of Reynolds Wrap Release Non-Stick Foil with a grilling fork. Place foil sheet on grill grate with non-stick (dull) side toward food. Immediately place ribs on foil.

BRUSH ribs with barbecue sauce. **CONTINUE GRILLING** uncovered 10 to 15 minutes, brushing with remaining sauce and turning every 5 minutes.

Makes 5 to 6 servings

Baked Fiesta Enchiladas

Prep Time: 25 minutes ■ Cook Time: 20 minutes

Reynolds Wrap® Release® Non-Stick Foil
1   **medium red bell pepper, chopped**
1   **package (8 ounces) sliced fresh mushrooms**
½   **cup sliced green onions**
1   **tablespoon vegetable or olive oil**
1   **cup sour cream**
1   **can (10¾ ounces) cream of chicken soup, undiluted**
1   **package (8 ounces) shredded sharp Cheddar cheese, divided**
1   **jar (2½ ounces) sliced ripe olives, drained (optional)**
2   **cups chopped cooked chicken or turkey**
6   **(8- to 10-inch) spinach, tomato or flour tortillas**
1   **jar (16 ounces) salsa**
    Sour cream and chopped fresh cilantro (optional)

PREHEAT oven to 350°F. For easy cleanup, line 13×9×2-inch baking pan with Reynolds Wrap Release Non-Stick Foil with non-stick (dull) side toward food; set aside.

COMBINE red pepper, mushrooms, onions and oil in medium saucepan. Over medium-high heat, stir and cook until pepper and mushrooms are tender; drain. Add sour cream, soup and half of cheese and olives. Stir in chicken.

SPOON about ¼ to 1 cup filling down center of tortillas, roll up and place side by side in foil-lined pan. Top with salsa and remaining cheese.

BAKE 20 to 25 minutes or until thoroughly heated. Top with sour cream and chopped fresh cilantro, if desired.

Makes 6 servings

Herbed Vegetable Packet

Baked Apple Cranberry Stuffing

Herb Roasted Holiday Turkey

Strawberries and Cream Cake

Holidays and Special
Occasions

Lemon Blueberry Shortcakes

Prep Time: 20 minutes ■ Cook Time: 17 minutes

24 Reynolds® Foil Baking Cups
1 package (18.25 ounces) vanilla or yellow cake mix
1 jar (10 ounces) lemon curd
**1 container (8 ounces) frozen whipped topping, thawed, divided
   Fresh blueberries or raspberries**

PREHEAT oven to 350°F. Place Reynolds Foil Baking Cups on cookie sheet with sides; set aside.

PREPARE cake mix following package directions for 24 cupcakes. Spoon cake batter into baking cups.

BAKE 17 to 22 minutes. Cool.

MIX lemon curd and 1 cup whipped topping in a medium bowl until well blended; set aside.

CUT the top off of each shortcake; set aside. Spoon about 1 tablespoon lemon mixture onto each shortcake; top with blueberries. Place top of shortcake over blueberries. Serve with remaining whipped topping.

Makes 24 servings

Herb Roasted Holiday Turkey

Prep Time: 15 minutes ■ Cook Time: 2 to 3½ hours

- 1 **Reynolds® Oven Bag, Turkey Size**
- 1 **tablespoon all-purpose flour**
- 2 **stalks celery, sliced**
- 1 **medium onion, sliced**
- 1 **(12- to 24-pound) turkey, thawed**
  Vegetable oil
- 1 **tablespoon dried sage**
- 1 **teaspoon dried thyme**
- 1 **teaspoon dried rosemary**
- 1 **teaspoon seasoned salt**

PREHEAT oven to 350°F.

SHAKE flour in Reynolds Oven Bag; place in large roasting pan at least two inches deep. If desired, spray inside of bag with nonstick spray to reduce sticking.

ADD vegetables to oven bag. Remove neck and giblets from turkey. Rinse turkey; pat dry. Brush turkey with oil. Combine sage, thyme, rosemary and seasoned salt on a sheet of wax paper. Sprinkle and rub herb mixture over turkey, turning to coat evenly.

PLACE turkey in oven bag on top of vegetables.

CLOSE oven bag with nylon tie; cut six ½-inch slits in top. Insert meat thermometer through slit in bag into thickest part of inner thigh not touching the bone. Tuck ends of bag in pan.

BAKE 2 to 2½ hours for a 12- to 16-pound turkey, 2½ to 3 hours for a 16- to 20-pound turkey, and 3 to 3½ hours for a 20- to 24-pound turkey, or until meat thermometer reads 180°F. For easy slicing, let stand in oven bag 15 minutes before opening.

REYNOLDS KITCHENS TIPS:

- *For stuffed turkey: Lightly stuff turkey with your favorite stuffing before brushing with oil. Add ½ hour to bake time.*
- *Estimate 1 pound per person for generous servings with leftovers.*

Makes 15 to 30 (3-ounce) servings

Herbed Vegetable Packet

Prep Time: 12 minutes ■ Cook Time: 20 minutes

1 **sheet (18×24 inches) Reynolds Wrap® Heavy Duty Aluminum Foil**
1 **small onion, thinly sliced**
3 **cups broccoli florets**
2 **medium carrots, thinly sliced**
1 **medium yellow squash or zucchini, sliced**
1 **teaspoon dried basil**
1 **teaspoon garlic salt**
2 **ice cubes**
2 **tablespoons butter OR olive oil**

PREHEAT oven to 450°F **OR** grill to medium-high.

CENTER vegetables on sheet of Reynolds Wrap Heavy Duty Aluminum Foil. Sprinkle with seasonings. Top with ice cubes and butter.

BRING up foil sides. Double fold top and ends to seal making one large foil packet, leaving room for heat circulation inside.

BAKE 20 to 25 minutes on a cookie sheet in oven **OR GRILL** 15 to 20 minutes in covered grill.

Makes 4 to 6 servings

"Non-Sticky" Buns

Prep Time: 8 minutes ■ Cook Time: 25 minutes

Reynolds Wrap® Release® Non-Stick Foil
½ **cup packed brown sugar**
3 **tablespoons butter OR margarine, melted**
2 **tablespoons light corn syrup**
½ **cup coarsely chopped pecans**
2 **cans (about 1 pound *each*) refrigerated big cinnamon rolls**

PREHEAT oven to 350°F. Line a 13×9×2-inch baking pan with Reynolds Wrap Release Non-Stick Foil with non-stick (dull) side facing up.

COMBINE brown sugar, butter and corn syrup; pour mixture into foil-lined pan. Sprinkle evenly with pecans. Place cinnamon rolls on top of syrup.

BAKE 25 to 29 minutes or until rolls are golden brown. Let stand 5 minutes. Invert onto platter. Remove foil. Serve warm.

REYNOLDS KITCHENS TIP:

The quickest way to line a pan is to flip the pan upside down. Press a sheet of Reynolds Wrap Release Non-Stick Foil around pan with non-stick (dull) side facing down. Remove foil. Flip pan upright and drop foil inside. Non-stick (dull) side should be facing up. Crimp foil edges to rim of pan.

Makes 10 servings

Brown Sugar Roasted Carrots

Prep Time: 8 minutes ■ Cook Time: 22 minutes

Reynolds Wrap® Release® Non-Stick Foil
1 **package (32 ounces) peeled baby carrots**
½ **cup packed dark brown sugar**
1 **tablespoon butter, melted**
1 **teaspoon grated orange peel**
½ **teaspoon 5-spice powder**
½ **teaspoon salt**
½ **cup pecan pieces**
  Orange peel (optional)

PREHEAT oven to 500°F. Line a 10½×15½×1-inch baking pan with Reynolds Wrap Release Non-Stick Foil with non-stick (dull) side toward food; set aside.

PLACE carrots in a single layer in foil-lined pan. Combine brown sugar, butter, orange peel, 5-spice powder and salt in a small bowl. Sprinkle brown sugar mixture evenly over carrots.

BAKE 20 minutes; stirring once. Sprinkle with pecans; bake 2 to 3 minutes longer or until carrots are tender and glazed. Garnish with more orange peel, if desired.

Makes 8 servings

Old-Fashioned Apple Pie

Prep Time: 25 minutes   ■   Cook Time: 45 minutes

Reynolds® Parchment Paper
Pastry for 9-inch deep dish, double crust pie
4 to 5 cups (3 pounds) tart cooking apples, peeled, cored and sliced
1¼ cups sugar
⅓ cup all-purpose flour
1 teaspoon ground cinnamon
1 tablespoon butter OR margarine
2 teaspoons milk
½ teaspoon sugar

PREHEAT oven to 350°F.

PREPARE pastry. Roll out half of dough to ⅛-inch thickness on a sheet of lightly floured Reynolds Parchment Paper. Place in nine-inch deep dish pie plate; set aside.

COMBINE apples, sugar, flour and cinnamon in a large mixing bowl; mix to coat apples thoroughly. Spoon mixture evenly into pie crust; top with butter.

ROLL remaining dough for top crust to ⅛-inch thickness on a lightly floured sheet of parchment paper. Place on top of pie. Trim off excess dough along edges. Fold edges under and crimp. Cut design in center to allow steam to escape. Brush dough lightly with milk; sprinkle with sugar.

BAKE 45 to 50 minutes or until crust is golden brown. Serve warm.

REYNOLDS KITCHENS TIP:

• *Easy Lattice Top: Start by placing 6 dough strips crosswise over the filling. Fold back every other strip a little past the center. Place another strip lengthwise on top of the flat strips. Unfold the strips to lay flat. Fold back the alternate crosswise strips and add another lengthwise strip. Continue weaving lattice, folding back alternate crosswise strips before adding each lengthwise strip, until lattice is complete.*

Makes 8 to 10 servings

Basil Appetizer Cheesecakes

Prep Time: 15 minutes   ■   Bake Time: 12 minutes

- 24 Reynolds® Mini Foil Baking Cups
- 2 packages (8 ounces *each*) neufchâtel (⅓ less fat) cream cheese, softened
- 1 tablespoon fresh lemon juice
- ¼ teaspoon salt
- 1 cup oil packed sun dried tomatoes, drained and chopped
- 2 eggs
- 2 tablespoons chopped fresh basil
- 1 clove garlic, minced
- ¼ cup finely crushed wheat crackers
- ¼ cup finely chopped walnuts
  Fresh basil leaves (optional)
  Assorted crackers

PREHEAT oven to 350°F. Place 24 Reynolds Mini Foil Baking Cups on a cookie sheet with sides. Spray baking cups with non-stick spray; set aside.

BEAT cream cheese, lemon juice and salt in medium bowl just until smooth with an electric mixer at medium speed. Add tomatoes, eggs, basil and garlic; beat on low speed, just until blended.

SPOON one heaping tablespoon cream cheese mixture into each baking cup.

COMBINE cracker crumbs and walnuts in a small bowl. Spoon about 1 teaspoon crumb mixture onto cheesecakes.

BAKE 12 to 14 minutes or until cheesecakes are set in center. Cool 15 minutes. Cover with Reynolds Plastic Wrap and refrigerate until serving time. Garnish with fresh basil leaves, if desired. Serve with crackers.

Makes 24 appetizer cheesecakes

Honey Almond Ambrosia Salad

Prep Time: 15 minutes ■ Chill Time: 3 hours

Reynolds® Plastic Wrap
1 **can (20 ounces) pineapple chunks in juice
   (drain and reserve ⅓ cup juice)**
1 **tablespoon honey**
½ **teaspoon almond extract**
½ **teaspoon grated orange peel**
1 **can (15 ounces) mandarin orange segments, drained
   OR 3 small oranges, peeled and sliced**
1 **container (16 ounces) strawberries, hulled and halved**
1 **cup miniature marshmallows**
1 **cup maraschino cherries (optional)**
½ **cup shredded coconut**

COMBINE the reserved pineapple juice, honey, almond extract and orange peel in a small bowl; set aside.

PLACE pineapple chunks, orange segments, strawberries, marshmallows and cherries, if desired, in 2-quart glass bowl. Drizzle with pineapple juice mixture.

COVER bowl with Reynolds Plastic Wrap and refrigerate until chilled, about 3 hours.

JUST before serving, sprinkle with coconut and toss gently.

Makes 6 to 8 servings

Cranberry Apple Sweet Potato Packet

Prep Time: 15 minutes   ■   Cook Time: 25 minutes

1 **sheet (18×24 inches) Reynolds Wrap® Heavy Duty Aluminum Foil**
4 **medium sweet potatoes (1½ pounds), peeled and cut into ¼-inch-thick slices**
2 **Granny Smith or Golden Delicious apples, cored, thinly sliced into rings**
½ **cup dried sweetened cranberries or raisins**
½ **cup packed brown sugar**
3 **tablespoons butter OR margarine, melted**
½ **teaspoon ground cinnamon**

PREHEAT oven to 450°F **OR** grill to medium-high.

CENTER sweet potatoes, apples and cranberries on sheet of Reynolds Wrap Heavy Duty Aluminum Foil. Sprinkle with brown sugar. Combine butter and cinnamon; drizzle over brown sugar.

BRING up foil sides. Double fold top and ends to seal making one large foil packet, leaving room for heat circulation inside.

BAKE 25 to 30 minutes on a cookie sheet in oven **OR GRILL** 20 to 25 minutes in covered grill until sweet potatoes are tender.

Makes 5 to 6 servings

Chili-Lime Pork with Sweet Potatoes

Prep Time: 20 minutes　■　Cook Time: 1 hour

- 1 **Reynolds® Oven Bag, Large Size**
- 1 **tablespoon all-purpose flour**
- 3 **tablespoons honey**
- 2 **tablespoons chili powder**
- 2 **teaspoons grated lime peel**
- 1 **(2½ pound) boneless top loin pork roast**
- 3 **medium sweet potatoes, peeled, cut into quarters**

PREHEAT oven to 325°F.

SHAKE flour in Reynolds Oven Bag; place in 13×9×2-inch or larger baking pan at least two inches deep.

COMBINE honey, chili powder and lime peel in a bowl; set aside. Pat surface of pork roast dry. Spread half of chili mixture evenly over bottom of pork. Add pork to oven bag; spread remaining chili mixture over top of pork. Arrange sweet potatoes around pork in an even layer in bag.

CLOSE oven bag with nylon tie; cut six ½-inch slits in top. Tuck ends of bag in pan.

BAKE 1 to 1¼ hours or until meat thermometer reads 160°F. Let stand in oven bag 5 minutes. To serve, place sliced pork on a serving platter. Arrange sweet potatoes around pork. Spoon juices over pork and sweet potatoes.

Makes 8 (3-ounce) servings

Baked Apple Cranberry Stuffing

Prep Time: 20 minutes ■ Cook Time: 35 minutes

Reynolds Wrap® Release® Non-Stick Foil
3 **tablespoons butter OR margarine**
2 **cups sliced celery**
1 **cup chopped onion**
1 **bag (14 ounces) cubed herb-seasoned stuffing**
1 **medium Granny Smith apple, chopped**
1 **cup dried sweetened cranberries**
2¼ **cups chicken broth**

PREHEAT oven to 350°F. Line a 13×9×2-inch baking pan with Reynolds Wrap Release Non-Stick Foil with non-stick (dull) side toward food; set aside.

MELT butter in saucepan. Add celery and onion; cook until tender **OR** place butter in a microwave-safe dish. Melt butter on HIGH, 1 to 2 minutes. Add celery and onion. Microwave on HIGH until tender, 5 to 8 minutes; set aside.

COMBINE stuffing, apple, dried cranberries and celery mixture in a large bowl. Gradually add broth to stuffing mixture, tossing until moistened. Spoon stuffing into foil-lined pan.

BAKE 35 to 40 minutes or until brown on top.

Makes 8 to 10 servings

Strawberries and Cream Cake

Prep Time: 30 minutes ■ Cook Time: 18 minutes

Reynolds® Parchment Paper
1   **package (18.25 ounces) yellow cake mix**
1   **cup milk**
½   **cup butter, melted**
3   **eggs**
2   **teaspoons vanilla extract**

FILLING:
1   **package (8 ounces) cream cheese, softened**
1   **cup powdered sugar**
½   **teaspoon vanilla extract**
1   **container (12 ounces) frozen whipped topping, thawed**
1   **container (16 ounces) fresh strawberries, hulled and sliced, divided**

PREHEAT oven to 350°F. Line the bottom of three eight-inch cake pans with Reynolds Parchment Paper; set aside.

BEAT cake mix, milk, butter, eggs and vanilla in a large bowl with electric mixer at low speed 30 seconds. Then beat on medium speed 2 minutes, scraping bowl occasionally. Divide batter evenly between parchment paper-lined cake pans.

BAKE 18 to 22 minutes or until toothpick inserted into centers comes out clean. Cool 10 minutes in pan. Invert cake layers onto a cooling rack; peel off parchment paper. Cool completely before filling and frosting.

FOR FILLING, beat cream cheese, powdered sugar and vanilla until smooth. Fold in whipped topping. Place one cake layer on a cake platter. Spread 1 cup of filling evenly over top of cake. Arrange one-third of strawberry slices over filling. Repeat with another cake layer, 1 cup of filling and one-third of strawberry slices. Top with remaining cake layer. Frost with remaining filling; top with remaining strawberries. Refrigerate until ready to serve. Garnish with strawberry fans.

REYNOLDS KITCHENS TIP:

To make strawberry fans, cut ⅛-inch slices from tip of strawberry to stem without cutting through. Fan out slices and place around edge of platter or on top of cake.

Makes 12 servings

Holiday Ham

Prep Time: 10 minutes ■ Cook Time: 2 hours

1 **Reynolds® Oven Bag, Turkey Size**
1 **tablespoon all-purpose flour**
1 **(8 to 10 pounds) fully-cooked bone-in ham half**
   Whole cloves (optional)

PREHEAT oven to 325°F.

SHAKE flour in Reynolds Oven Bag; place in large roasting pan at least two inches deep. Trim skin and excess fat from ham, leaving a thin layer of fat. If desired, score ham by lightly cutting diamond shapes into surface; insert cloves into center of diamonds, if desired.

PLACE ham in oven bag.

CLOSE oven bag with nylon tie; cut six ½-inch slits in top. Insert meat thermometer through slit in bag into thickest part of ham, not touching bone. Tuck ends of bag into pan.

BAKE 2 to 2½ hours or until meat thermometer reads 140°F. Let stand in oven bag 10 minutes before slicing.

Makes 24 to 30 (3-ounce) servings

Slow Cooker Smashed Potatoes

Prep Time: 15 minutes ▪ Cook Time: 6 hours

1   **Reynolds® Slow Cooker Liner**
3   **pounds medium potatoes, peeled and cut into large cubes**
2   **to 4 cloves garlic, minced**
1   **teaspoon salt**
½   **teaspoon black pepper**
1   **cup water**
½   **cup milk**
½   **cup butter OR margarine, melted**

OPEN Reynolds Slow Cooker Liner and place it inside a 5- to 6½-quart slow cooker bowl. Fit liner snugly against the bottom and sides of bowl; pull top of liner over rim of bowl.

PLACE potatoes in slow cooker liner; sprinkle with garlic, salt and pepper. Pour water over potatoes. Place lid on slow cooker.

COOK on LOW for 6 to 7 hours **OR** on HIGH for 3 to 4 hours or until potatoes are tender.

CAREFULLY remove lid to allow steam to escape. Gently mash potatoes into smaller pieces using a potato masher or back of a wooden or plastic spoon. Add milk and butter; stir gently. Serve warm potatoes directly from slow cooker liner. Do not lift or transport liner with food inside. Cool slow cooker completely; remove liner and toss.

REYNOLDS KITCHENS TIP:
Reynolds Slow Cooker Liners are great for reheating leftover Smashed Potatoes. Place potatoes in a lined-slow cooker. Heat on HIGH for 1 to 2 hours or until potatoes are hot.

Makes 8 to 9 servings

Chocolate Cappuccino Cupcakes

Prep Time: 10 minutes ■ Cook Time: 17 minutes

24 **Reynolds® Baking Cups**
1 **package (about 18 ounces) chocolate cake mix**
¼ **cup instant coffee, divided**
2 **teaspoons hot water**
1 **container (16 ounces) ready-to-spread cream cheese frosting**
½ **cup semi-sweet chocolate chips**
2 **teaspoons vegetable oil**

PREHEAT oven to 350°F. Place Reynolds Baking Cups in muffin pans; set aside.
Prepare cake mix following package directions for 24 cupcakes, adding
2 tablespoons instant coffee before mixing. Spoon batter into baking cups.

BAKE 17 to 22 minutes. Cool.

DISSOLVE remaining instant coffee in hot water in a bowl. Stir frosting into
coffee mixture until smooth. Frost cupcakes.

MICROWAVE chocolate chips and oil on HIGH power in a small microwave-safe
dish, 1 to 1½ minutes, stirring once, until chocolate is melted.

DRIZZLE melted chocolate over frosted cupcakes. Let stand until chocolate sets.

Makes 24 cupcakes

Yellow Squash, Tomato & Onion Packet

Prep Time: 16 minutes ■ Cook Time: 18 minutes

1 **sheet (18×24 inches) Reynolds Wrap® Heavy Duty Aluminum Foil**
1 **medium onion, chopped**
2 **medium yellow squash, cut into ¼-inch-thick slices**
4 **large Roma tomatoes, quartered**
¼ **cup chopped fresh basil**
   Salt and black pepper
⅓ **cup shredded Parmesan cheese**

PREHEAT oven to 450°F **OR** grill to medium-high.

CENTER onion on sheet of Reynolds Wrap Heavy Duty Aluminum Foil; top with yellow squash and tomatoes. Sprinkle with basil, salt and pepper.

BRING up foil sides. Double fold top and ends to seal making one large packet, leaving room for heat circulation inside.

BAKE 18 to 22 minutes on a cookie sheet in oven **OR GRILL** 13 to 15 minutes in covered grill. Open foil packet; sprinkle vegetables with cheese. Let stand about 3 minutes until cheese melts.

Makes 6 servings

Chocolate Dipped Macaroon Cookies

Prep Time: 15 minutes ■ Chill Time: 10 minutes

Reynolds® Cut-Rite® Wax Paper
1 **package (13 ounces) coconut macaroons (16 cookies)**
½ **cup semi-sweet chocolate chips**
½ **cup premium white chocolate chips**
Multi-colored sprinkles

LINE counter top with Reynolds Cut-Rite Wax Paper for easy cleanup.

PLACE semi-sweet chocolate chips in a microwave-safe bowl. Stirring every 30 seconds, microwave on HIGH power until chocolate is melted, 45 seconds to 1½ minutes. Repeat to melt premium white chips.

DIP the top half of eight of the macaroon cookies in melted semi-sweet chocolate; place on another sheet of wax paper. Immediately sprinkle melted chocolate with sprinkles. Refrigerate 10 to 15 minutes or until the melted chocolate sets.

DIP the top half of the remaining eight macaroon cookies in melted white chips; place on another sheet of wax paper. Immediately sprinkle melted white chips with sprinkles. Refrigerate 10 to 15 minutes or until the melted chips set.

MAKE a gift basket by lining a small basket with wax paper.

REYNOLDS KITCHENS TIP:
For Cookie Bundles, when chocolate sets, stack two macaroon cookies. Wrap each stack with Reynolds® Color Plastic Wrap. Tie the top of each bundle with ribbon. Put the bundles in a holiday container or gift basket lined with Reynolds® Cut-Rite® Wax Paper.

Makes 16 servings

Standing Rib Roast & Three Potato Bake

Prep Time: 15 minutes ■ Cook Time: 2 hours

- 1 **Reynolds® Oven Bag, Large Size**
- 2 **tablespoons all-purpose flour**
- 1½ **teaspoons beef bouillon granules**
- 1½ **teaspoons dried rosemary, crushed**
- 1 **teaspoon lemon pepper**
- 2 **large cloves garlic, minced**
- 1 **(5- to 6-pound) bone-in beef rib roast**
- 2 **medium sweet potatoes, peeled, halved**
- 2 **small russet potatoes, peeled, halved**
- 2 **small Yukon Gold potatoes, peeled, halved**
  Salt and black pepper to taste

PREHEAT oven to 325°F.

SHAKE flour in Reynolds Oven Bag; place in 13×9×2-inch or larger baking pan at least two inches deep. Combine beef bouillon granules, rosemary, lemon pepper and garlic; rub onto surface of roast.

ADD roast, fat side up, to oven bag. Arrange potatoes around roast in an even layer in bag.

CLOSE oven bag with nylon tie; cut six ½-inch slits in top.

BAKE 2 to 2½ hours or until meat thermometer reads 145°F for rare. Remove potatoes from oven bag; place in serving bowl. Season with salt and pepper. Skim fat from sauce; season sauce with salt and pepper. Serve roast with vegetables and sauce.

Makes 10 to 12 servings

All American Ice Cream Cups   Back-to-School Cupcakes

Candy Bar Cupcakes   **PBJ Puzzle Sandwich**

Cooking for Kids

PBJ Puzzle Sandwich

Prep Time: 10 minutes

4 Reynolds® Wrappers™ Pop-Up Foil Sheets
½ cup creamy peanut butter
¼ cup dried fruit bits
¼ cup apricot preserves or strawberry jam
8 slices white or whole wheat bread

COMBINE peanut butter, fruit bits and preserves. Spread one-fourth of filling between two slices of bread.

CUT center of sandwich into fun shape using a cookie cutter. Use a knife to cut remaining sandwich into pieces to form a puzzle. Reassemble sandwich.

WRAP sandwich in one Reynolds Wrappers Pop-Up Foil Sheet. Repeat to make four sandwiches.

Makes 4 servings

Flower Pots and Shovels

Prep Time: 20 minutes

Reynolds® Clear and Color Plastic Wrap
8 white plastic spoons
½ cup premium white chocolate chips, melted
Multi-colored sprinkles
8 (9-ounce) clear plastic cups
8 (12-inch) chenille stems
2½ cups cold milk
1 package (5.9 ounces) instant chocolate pudding mix
32 chocolate sandwich cookies, crushed and divided
Caramel popcorn, crushed
Gummy worms

DIP plastic spoons into melted chips to coat; let excess drizzle off. Sprinkle with colored sprinkles. Place spoons on a wax paper-covered tray; refrigerate until hardened.

COVER coated spoons with Reynolds Clear Plastic Wrap. To make flower petals, wrap handles of spoons with Reynolds Color Plastic Wrap. Gather and twist plastic wrap around base of spoon; fluff ends and trim, if needed.

TO MAKE FLOWER POT HANDLES, make two small holes below rims on opposite sides of *each* plastic cup. Insert ends of chenille stems through holes; twist to secure handles.

BEAT milk and pudding mix in large bowl for 2 minutes with wire whisk; stir in 1 cup crushed cookies. Spoon 1 tablespoon crushed cookies into *each* plastic cup; top with pudding mixture. Insert handle of a spoon into center of pudding in *each* cup. Top pudding with remaining crushed cookies for dirt, crushed caramel popcorn for rocks and gummy worms. Chill, if desired.

Makes 8 desserts

Easy Broccoli Packet

Prep Time: 5 minutes ■ Cook Time: 12 minutes

1 sheet (18×24 inches) Reynolds Wrap® Heavy Duty Aluminum Foil
3 cups broccoli florets
⅓ cup Italian dressing

PREHEAT oven to 450°F **OR** grill to medium-high.

CENTER broccoli on sheet of Reynolds Wrap Heavy Duty Aluminum Foil; drizzle with dressing.

BRING up foil sides. Double fold top and ends to form one large foil packet, leaving room for heat circulation inside.

BAKE 12 to 15 minutes on a cookie sheet in oven **OR GRILL** 10 to 12 minutes in covered grill until broccoli is crisp-tender.

Makes 4 servings

Slow Cooker Sloppy Joes

Prep Time: 20 minutes ■ Cook Time: 6 hours

- 1 Reynolds® Slow Cooker Liner
- 2 pounds ground beef
- 1 large onion, chopped
- 1 medium green bell pepper, chopped
- 2 cups ketchup
- 1 cup barbecue sauce
- 1 to 2 tablespoons *each* vinegar and Worcestershire sauce (optional)
- 1 tablespoon prepared mustard
- 8 to 10 sandwich buns

OPEN Reynolds Slow Cooker Liner and place it inside a 5- to 6½-quart slow cooker bowl. Fit liner snugly against the bottom and sides of bowl; pull top of liner over rim of bowl.

BROWN ground beef, onion and bell pepper in a large skillet over medium-high heat, stirring occasionally, until beef is no longer pink. Drain well.

PLACE beef mixture in slow cooker liner. Combine ketchup, barbecue sauce, vinegar, Worcestershire sauce and mustard in a medium bowl; pour over beef mixture. Place lid on slow cooker.

COOK on LOW for 6 to 7 hours **OR** on HIGH for 3 to 3½ hours or until heated through.

CAREFULLY remove lid to allow steam to escape. Gently stir Sloppy Joe mixture; spoon over sandwich buns. Do not lift or transport liner with food inside. Cool slow cooker completely; remove liner and toss.

Makes 8 to 10 servings

REYNOLDS KITCHENS TIP:

This recipe makes enough to serve a crowd or to save half for a second meal. Reheat leftovers and serve over rice or pasta. Or serve over tortilla chips topped with shredded lettuce and cheese.

Baked Spaghetti

Prep Time: 20 minutes ■ Cook Time: 45 minutes

Reynolds Wrap® Release® Non-Stick Foil
1 **package (8 ounces) spaghetti, cooked and drained**
2 **tablespoons butter OR olive oil**
1 **cup grated Parmesan cheese, divided**
1 **container (24 ounces) ricotta cheese OR cottage cheese**
1 **pound ground beef**
1 **jar (about 28 ounces) chunky garden-style pasta sauce**
1 **package (8 ounces) shredded mozzarella cheese**

PREHEAT oven to 400°F. Line a 13×9×2-inch baking pan with Reynolds Wrap Release Non-Stick Foil with non-stick (dull) side toward food.

COMBINE hot cooked spaghetti with butter; stir until butter melts and coats spaghetti. Add ½ cup Parmesan cheese; stir to coat. Arrange spaghetti in an even layer in foil-lined pan. Spread ricotta cheese over spaghetti. Sprinkle with ¼ cup Parmesan cheese. Brown ground beef, drain; add pasta sauce and heat until bubbly. Spoon over cheeses. Top with mozzarella cheese and remaining ¼ cup Parmesan cheese.

COVER with non-stick foil with dull side toward food. Bake 30 minutes. Remove foil cover and continue baking 15 minutes or until cheese is lightly browned. Let stand 10 minutes before serving.

Makes 6 servings

Candy Bar Cupcakes

Prep Time: 10 minutes   ■   Bake Time: 17 minutes

24 **Reynolds® Pastels Baking Cups**
 1 **package (about 18 ounces) chocolate cake mix**
 1 **container (16 ounces) vanilla ready-to-spread frosting**
    Assorted candy bars, crushed or finely chopped

PREHEAT oven to 350°F. Place Reynolds Pastels Baking Cups in muffin pans; set aside.

PREPARE cake mix following package directions for 24 cupcakes. Spoon cake batter into baking cups.

BAKE 17 to 22 minutes. Cool.

FROST cupcakes with frosting. Decorate with crushed candy.

Makes 24 cupcakes

REYNOLDS KITCHENS TIP:
A size 20 ice cream scoop is a great tool for filling baking cups with cake batter.

Back-to-School Cupcakes

Prep Time: 15 minutes ■ Cook Time: 17 minutes

- 24 Reynolds® Pastels Baking Cups
- 1 package (18.25 ounces) any flavor cake mix
- 1 container (16 ounces) ready-to-spread white frosting
  Food colors
  Decorating icing
  Pretzel rods
  Green taffy

PREHEAT oven to 350°F. Place Reynolds Pastels Baking Cups in muffin pans; set aside.

PREPARE cake mix following package directions for 24 cupcakes. Spoon cake batter into baking cups.

BAKE 17 to 22 minutes. Cool.

TINT frosting to desired color; frost cupcakes. Write messages on cupcakes with decorating icing. To make apple, frost with red tinted frosting. Insert broken pretzel rod for stem and green taffy for leaf. Repeat for remaining cupcakes.

Makes 24 cupcakes

All-American Ice Cream Cups

Prep Time: 15 minutes ■ Chill Time: 1 hour

18 **Reynolds® Foil Baking Cups**
 2 **cups loosely packed coconut macaroon cookie crumbs
    (10 cookies, 2-inch diameter)**
¼ **cup apricot preserves**
½ **teaspoon almond extract**
½ **gallon vanilla ice cream, slightly softened**
18 **maraschino cherries**
½ **cup sliced almonds
    Reynolds Wrap® Heavy Duty Aluminum Foil**

PLACE Reynolds Foil Baking Cups in muffin pans; set aside.

COMBINE cookie crumbs, apricot preserves and almond extract in a bowl. Stir with fork until crumbs are coated. Press one rounded tablespoon crumb mixture into bottom of each baking cup.

PLACE one scoop of ice cream into each baking cup. Top each dessert with a cherry and an almond slice.

FREEZE until serving time. For freezer storage, cover muffin pans tightly with Reynolds Wrap Heavy Duty Aluminum Foil.

Makes 18 desserts

Water Fun Cake

Prep Time: 30 minutes   ■   Cook Time: 15 minutes

Reynolds® Color Plastic Wrap, Blue and Green
- 1 package (about 18 ounces) cake mix
- 1 white cardboard (25×16 inches) OR purchased sheet cake board
- 1½ containers (16 ounces *each*) prepared vanilla frosting
- 1 to 2 tablespoons graham cracker crumbs
- 6 fish graham snacks OR gummy fish candies
- 12 teddy bear-shaped graham snacks
- 5 gummy ring-shaped candies
- 2 sticks fruit-striped chewing gum
- 2 sugar wafers
- 4 pull-apart licorice strings
- 1 fruit roll-up
- 1 licorice twist, cut in half
- 1 gum ball
- 2 paper drink umbrellas

PREHEAT oven to 350°F. Spray a 15½×10½×1-inch baking pan with nonstick spray. Prepare cake mix following package directions. Pour batter into pan. Bake 15 to 20 minutes or until toothpick inserted into center comes out clean. Cool.

COVER white cardboard with Reynolds Blue Plastic Wrap, taping to back. Center cake on cardboard; frost. For beach, sprinkle half of cake very lightly with graham cracker crumbs. For water, cover remaining half of cake with blue plastic wrap. Arrange fish snacks on top of plastic wrap. Cover fish with another layer of blue plastic wrap.

DECORATE cake as desired for water fun. Use teddy bear-shaped graham snacks for swimmers. Use gummy ring-shaped candies for inner tubes. Cut fruit-striped chewing gum for beach towels. Use two sugar wafers for diving board; glue together with frosting. Add licorice strings for handrails; attach to diving board with frosting. For sliding board; press pull-apart licorice strings to long edges of a three-inch strip of fruit roll-up. Bend and insert into cake. For palm tree, tear off two (twelve-inch) sheets of green plastic wrap. Fold *each* into a two-inch-wide strip; trim and cut fringe to make leaves. Crisscross strips; cut an "X" in center. Slide over end of licorice twist; insert into cake. Add gum ball and paper umbrellas.

Makes 24 servings

Brownie Pizza

Prep Time: 15 minutes ■ Cook Time: 20 minutes

Reynolds® Parchment Paper
1 **package (about 19 ounces) fudge brownie mix**
1 **container (16 ounces) ready-to-spread frosting, any flavor**
  Chocolate coated candies, colored sprinkles, mini marshmallows or nuts

PREHEAT oven to 350°F. Line a large cookie sheet with Reynolds Parchment Paper. Trace a twelve-inch circle on parchment paper.

PREPARE brownie mix following package directions for fudgy brownies. Pour batter in center of parchment paper on cookie sheet; spread batter evenly inside circle.

BAKE 20 to 22 minutes or until wooden pick inserted into center comes out clean. Cool on wire rack.

FROST brownie, leaving a one-inch border unfrosted for the "pizza crust." Decorate with candies, sprinkles, marshmallows or nuts.

Makes 12 servings

After School Snack Mix

Prep Time: 10 minutes   ■   Cook Time: 45 minutes

Reynolds Wrap® Release® Non-Stick Foil
3 **cups toasted whole grain oat cereal**
3 **cups miniature pretzel twists**
2 **cups miniature cinnamon bear-shaped graham snacks**
½ **cup pancake syrup**
2 **tablespoons melted butter OR margarine**
1 **teaspoon ground cinnamon**
1 **package (14.5 ounces) candy coated chocolate candies**
24 **Reynolds® Baking Cups**

PREHEAT oven to 275°F. Line a 15×10½×1-inch baking pan with Reynolds Wrap Release Non-Stick Foil with non-stick (dull) side toward food; set aside.

COMBINE cereal, pretzels and graham snacks in a large bowl. Combine syrup, butter and cinnamon in another bowl. Pour over cereal mixture; tossing to coat evenly. Spread cereal mixture in foil-lined pan.

BAKE 45 minutes. Cool mixture in baking pan on wire rack. Lift foil to break mixture apart. Stir in chocolate candies. Place a heaping one-third cup mixture into *each* Reynolds Baking Cup.

Makes 24 servings

Pizzeria Chicken Packets

Prep Time: 20 minutes ■ Cook Time: 18 minutes

4 sheets (12×18 inches *each*) Reynolds Wrap® Release®
      Non-Stick Foil
4 boneless, skinless chicken breast halves (1 to 1¼ pounds)
1 cup pizza or spaghetti sauce
1 cup shredded low-fat mozzarella cheese
20 slices turkey pepperoni
1 medium green bell pepper, chopped
1 small onion, chopped

PREHEAT oven to 450°F **OR** grill to medium-high.

CENTER one chicken breast half on *each* sheet of Reynolds Wrap Release Non-Stick Foil with non-stick (dull) side toward food. Spoon pizza sauce over chicken. Sprinkle with cheese; top with pepperoni, green pepper and onion.

BRING up foil sides. Double fold top and ends to seal packet, leaving room for heat circulation inside. Repeat to make four packets.

BAKE 18 to 22 minutes on a cookie sheet in oven **OR GRILL** 10 to 12 minutes in covered grill.

Makes 4 servings

REYNOLDS KITCHENS TIP:

Substitute your favorite pizza toppings for the pepperoni, green pepper and onion. If desired, sprinkle with grated Parmesan cheese before serving.

Party Cheesecakes

Prep Time: 20 minutes   ■   Cook Time: 20 minutes

- 16 Reynolds® Foil Baking Cups OR 32 Reynolds® Mini Foil Baking Cups
- 25 chocolate sandwich cookies, crushed
- ⅓ cup butter OR margarine, melted
- 2 packages (8 ounces *each*) cream cheese, softened
- ½ cup sugar
- 2 eggs
- ½ teaspoon vanilla extract
- ¾ cup mini chocolate chips, divided
- 1 teaspoon vegetable oil (do not use butter or margarine)

PREHEAT oven to 350°F. Place Reynolds Foil Baking Cups OR Reynolds Mini Foil Baking Cups on cookie sheets with sides; set aside.

COMBINE chocolate cookie crumbs and butter. Press one rounded tablespoon crumb mixture into bottom of each foil baking cup. (Press 1 ½ teaspoons in bottom of each mini foil baking cup.)

BEAT cream cheese, sugar, eggs and vanilla extract until smooth in bowl, with electric mixer. Stir in ½ cup chocolate chips. Spoon mixture evenly into baking cups, filling each cup ¾ full.

BAKE 20 to 25 minutes. (Bake mini cheesecakes 16 to 18 minutes.) Cool. For chocolate drizzle, place remaining ¼ cup chocolate chips and oil in a microwave safe bowl. Microwave on MEDIUM (50% power) until melted and mixture can be stirred smooth, 1 to 2 minutes. Drizzle over cooled cheesecakes. Refrigerate at least 2 hours before serving.

MAKES 16 individual or 32 mini cheesecakes

REYNOLDS KITCHENS TIP:

If using Mini Foil Baking Cups, you may use small vanilla-flavored wafer cookies instead of making crumb crust. Place vanilla-flavored wafer cookies rounded side down in mini foil baking cups. Add filling and bake as directed above.

Cheese Fries

Prep Time: 8 minutes ■ Cook Time: 20 minutes

Reynolds Wrap® Release® Non-Stick Foil
½ **package (from a 32-ounce package) frozen crinkle-cut French fries**
2 **cups shredded sharp Cheddar cheese**
1 **small tomato, chopped**
2 **green onions, chopped**

PREHEAT oven to 450°F. Line a 15½×10½×1-inch baking pan with Reynolds Wrap Release Non-Stick Foil with non-stick (dull) side toward food.

BAKE French fries on foil-lined pan following package directions until crisp. Sprinkle with cheese, tomatoes and onions.

CONTINUE baking 3 to 4 minutes or until cheese is melted.

Makes 6 servings

California Grilled Pizza

Prep Time: 10 minutes   ■   Grill Time: 5 minutes

- 2 **Reynolds® Wrappers™ Pop-Up Foil Sheets**
- 2 **pizza crusts (8 inches *each*)**
- 1 **teaspoon chopped garlic (about 2 cloves)**
- ½ **of a medium red onion, cut into thin strips**
- 2 **tablespoons olive oil**
- 2 **plum tomatoes, thinly sliced**
- ½ **jar (from a 6-ounce jar) marinated artichoke hearts, thinly sliced**
- 4 **to 6 baby portobello mushrooms, thinly sliced**
- 2 **tablespoons chopped fresh basil**
- ½ **cup shredded mozzarella cheese**

PREHEAT grill to medium-high.

PLACE *each* pizza crust on a Reynolds Wrappers Pop-Up Foil Sheet. In a small skillet over medium heat, cook garlic and onion in olive oil 2 to 3 minutes or until onion is softened.

BRUSH pizza crusts with olive oil mixture; arrange onion evenly on pizza. Top with tomatoes, artichoke hearts, mushrooms and basil. Brush mushrooms with marinade from artichokes. Sprinkle with cheese.

GRILL pizza on foil sheet in covered grill for 5 to 7 minutes or until cheese is melted.

Makes 4 servings

Birthday Cake Cupcakes

Prep Time: 20 minutes   ■   Cook Time: 20 minutes

- 24 **Reynolds® Baking Cups**
- 1 **package (18.25 ounces) natural vanilla or yellow cake mix**
- 1 **container (16 ounces) ready-to-spread white frosting**
- **Food colors**
- **Assorted sprinkles**
- 24 **large gumdrops**
- **Red peel-away string licorice**

PREHEAT oven to 350°F. Place Reynolds Baking Cups in muffin pans; set aside.

PREPARE cake mix following package directions for 24 cupcakes. Spoon cake batter into baking cups.

BAKE 20 to 25 minutes. Cool.

TINT frosting as desired. Frost cupcakes and decorate with sprinkles, if desired. To make "mini birthday cake", spread a small amount of frosting on the bottom of the gumdrop (the wider end). Cut a small strip of string licorice for the candle and press into frosting on gumdrop. Place on top of cupcake. Repeat for remaining cupcakes.

Makes 24 servings

Corn & Salsa Chicken Packets

Prep Time: 9 minutes ■ Cook Time: 18 minutes

- **4 sheets (12×18 inches *each*) Reynolds Wrap® Heavy Duty Aluminum Foil**
- **4 boneless, skinless chicken breast halves (1 to 1¼ pounds)**
- **1 cup chunky salsa**
- **1 can (15¼ ounces) whole kernel corn, drained**
- **1 cup shredded Cheddar cheese**

PREHEAT oven to 450°F **OR** grill to medium-high

CENTER one chicken breast half on *each* sheet of Reynolds Wrap Heavy Duty Aluminum Foil. Spoon salsa over chicken. Top with corn.

BRING up foil sides. Double fold top and ends to seal packet, leaving room for heat circulation inside. Repeat to make four packets.

BAKE 18 to 22 minutes on a cookie sheet in oven **OR GRILL** 12 to 15 minutes in covered grill. Sprinkle with cheese before serving.

REYNOLDS KITCHENS TIP:

Serve with tortilla chips.

Makes 4 servings

Favorite Chocolate Chip Cookies

Prep Time: 15 minutes ■ Cook Time: 10 minutes

Reynolds® Parchment Paper

- 2½ **cups all-purpose flour**
- 1 **teaspoon baking powder**
- 1 **teaspoon salt**
- ½ **teaspoon ground cinnamon (optional)**
- 1 **cup butter, softened**
- 1 **cup packed brown sugar**
- ½ **cup granulated sugar**
- 2 **eggs**
- 2 **teaspoons vanilla extract**
- 1 **package (12 ounces) OR 2 cups semi-sweet chocolate chips**
- 1 **cup coarsely chopped nuts**

PREHEAT oven to 350°F. Line cookie sheets with Reynolds Parchment Paper; set aside. On another sheet of parchment paper, combine flour, baking powder, salt and cinnamon; set aside.

BEAT together butter, brown sugar and granulated sugar in a large mixing bowl with an electric mixer until light and fluffy. Beat in eggs and vanilla.

ADD flour mixture gradually to butter mixture; beat until well blended. Stir in chocolate chips and nuts. Drop by rounded tablespoons onto parchment-lined cookie sheets.

BAKE 10 to 12 minutes or until lightly browned. Cool. If desired, wrap cookies in Reynolds® Wrappers™ Pop-Up Foil Sheets for lunch box and after school snacks.

Makes 3½ to 4 dozen cookies

Cajun Sausage & Beans Packets

Herbed Salmon Packets

Grilled Italian Vegetables

Kansas City Style Ribs

Great Grilling

Kansas City Style Ribs

Prep Time: 15 minutes ■ Grill Time: 45 minutes

- 2 **sheets (18×24 inches *each*) Reynolds Wrap® Heavy Duty Aluminum Foil**
- 3 **pounds baby back pork ribs**
- ½ **cup water**
- ½ **teaspoon liquid smoke**
- 2 **tablespoons butter OR vegetable oil**
- ½ **cup finely chopped onion**
- 2 **cups ketchup**
- ¼ **cup Worcestershire sauce**
- ¼ **cup cider vinegar**
- 1 **tablespoon prepared mustard**
- 1 **tablespoon molasses**
- ½ **teaspoon ground cumin**

PREHEAT grill to medium. Cut each rack of ribs into thirds. Center half of ribs in single layer on each sheet of Reynolds Wrap Heavy Duty Aluminum Foil.

BRING up foil sides. Double fold one end to seal. Through open end, add ¼ cup water and ¼ teaspoon liquid smoke. Double fold remaining end, leaving room for heat circulation inside packet. Repeat for second packet.

GRILL 45 minutes to 1 hour on medium in covered grill. Melt butter in medium saucepan over medium-high heat. Add onion and cook until tender. Add remaining ingredients. Simmer over medium-low heat 20 to 25 minutes while ribs steam in the foil packet. Remove steamed ribs carefully from foil. Place directly on grill.

BRUSH ribs generously with sauce. Continue grilling 10 to 15 minutes on medium in uncovered grill, brushing with sauce and turning every 5 minutes to cook evenly.

Makes 6 servings

Herbed Salmon Packets

Prep Time: 10 minutes ■ Grill Time: 10 minutes

- **4 sheets (12×18 inches *each*) Reynolds Wrap® Release® Non-Stick Foil**
- **4 salmon fillets (4 to 6 ounces *each*), thawed**
- **¼ cup chopped fresh parsley**
- **2 teaspoons dried dill weed**
- **1½ teaspoons sugar**
- **1½ teaspoons grated lime peel**
- **¾ teaspoon dry mustard**
- **½ teaspoon salt**
- **2 medium zucchini, sliced**
- **2 medium carrots, thinly sliced**

PREHEAT grill to medium-high **OR** oven to 450°F.

CENTER one salmon fillet on *each* sheet of Reynolds Wrap Release Non-Stick Foil with non-stick (dull) side toward food. Combine parsley, dill weed, sugar, lime peel, mustard and salt on a sheet of wax paper. Sprinkle and rub half of seasoning mixture over salmon, turning to coat evenly. Arrange vegetables around salmon. Sprinkle vegetables with remaining seasoning mixture.

BRING up foil sides. Double fold top and ends to seal packet, leaving room for heat circulation inside. Repeat to make four packets.

GRILL 10 to 12 minutes in covered grill **OR BAKE** 16 to 18 minutes on a cookie sheet in oven.

Makes 4 servings

Spicy Grilled Shrimp

Prep Time: 30 minutes ■ Grill Time: 4 minutes

Reynolds Wrap® Release® Non-Stick Foil
¼ **cup fresh lemon juice**
2 **tablespoons Worcestershire sauce**
4 **teaspoons seafood seasoning**
2 **teaspoons lemon pepper**
1 **teaspoon dried basil**
3 **to 4 cloves garlic, minced**
½ **cup vegetable oil**
1 **pound medium raw shrimp, peeled and deveined**

COMBINE lemon juice, Worcestershire sauce, seafood seasoning, lemon pepper, basil and garlic. Gradually add oil, stirring marinade until thickened. Reserve half of marinade for basting. Add shrimp to remaining marinade; stir to coat evenly. Cover shrimp with Reynolds Plastic Wrap; refrigerate 30 minutes. Drain shrimp; discard marinade.

PREHEAT grill to medium-high. Make drainage holes in a sheet of Reynolds Wrap Release Non-Stick Foil with a large grilling fork. Place foil sheet on grill grate with non-stick (dull) side toward food. Immediately arrange shrimp on foil.

GRILL uncovered 4 to 6 minutes, turning and basting once with reserved marinade, until shrimp are firm and pink.

REYNOLDS KITCHENS TIP:

For drainage holes, lay a sheet of Reynolds Wrap Release Non-Stick Foil over a cold grill grate, broiler pan or cooling rack. Make holes in the foil with a large grilling fork.

Makes 4 servings

Grilled Italian Vegetables

Prep Time: 15 minutes ■ Grill Time: 25 minutes

- 2 **sheets (18×20 inches *each*) Reynolds Wrap® Heavy Duty Aluminum Foil**
- 1 **medium red bell pepper, cut into strips**
- 1 **medium zucchini, thinly sliced**
- 1 **small red onion, thinly sliced**
- 8 **small whole mushrooms**
- 3 **Roma tomatoes, sliced ½ inch thick**
- 3 **cloves garlic, minced**
- 3 **tablespoons olive oil**
- 3 **tablespoons lemon juice**
- 1 **teaspoon dried basil**
- ½ **teaspoon seasoned salt**
- ¼ **teaspoon dried thyme**
- ¼ **cup grated Romano or Parmesan cheese (optional)**

PREHEAT grill to medium-high.

MAKE a Reynolds Do-It-Yourself (DIY) Grill Pan; place on a tray.

PLACE vegetables in DIY Grill Pan. Combine oil, lemon juice, basil, seasoned salt and thyme; drizzle over vegetables. Slide foil pan onto grill grate.

GRILL 25 to 30 minutes on medium-high in covered grill, stirring frequently. Slide foil pan from grill onto tray. If desired, sprinkle vegetables with grated cheese.

Makes 6 servings

REYNOLDS KITCHENS TIP:

To make a Reynolds Do-It-Yourself (DIY) Grill Pan, stack two sheets of Reynolds Wrap Heavy Duty Aluminum Foil. Flip a 13×9×2-inch pan upside down. Press sheets of foil around pan. Remove foil from pan; crimp edges to make a pan. Place DIY Grill Pan on a tray to transport to and from the grill.

Grilled Fajitas

Prep Time: 10 minutes ■ Grill Time: 8 minutes

- 2 **sheets (18×20 inches *each*) Reynolds Wrap® Heavy Duty Aluminum Foil**
- 1 **package (1 ounce) fajita seasoning mix**
- 1 **pound boneless beef top round steak OR 4 boneless, skinless chicken breast halves (1 to 1¼ pounds)**
- 1 **medium red or yellow bell pepper, cut into strips**
- 1 **medium green bell pepper, cut into strips**
- 1 **medium onion, cut into ¼-inch-thick slices**
- 1 **tablespoon vegetable oil**
- 8 **flour tortillas (8 inches *each*)**
  Salsa

PREPARE fajita seasoning mix following package directions and pour over steak or chicken in a bowl. Cover with Reynolds Wrap Heavy Duty Aluminum Foil. Refrigerate 1 to 2 hours.

PREHEAT grill to high. Make a Reynolds Do-It-Yourself (DIY) Grill Pan; place on a tray. Remove steak or chicken from marinade; discard marinade. Spread peppers and onion evenly in DIY Grill Pan; drizzle with oil. Slide pan onto grill grate. Place steak or chicken on grill grate beside pan.

GRILL 8 to 10 minutes in covered grill, turning frequently, until vegetables are crisp-tender.

TURN steak or chicken after 5 minutes. Slide foil pan from grill onto tray. Slice grilled steak or chicken into thin strips.

WRAP tortillas in foil; add to grill to heat while slicing steak or chicken. Serve beef or chicken, peppers and onions wrapped in warm tortillas with salsa.

Makes 4 servings

REYNOLDS KITCHENS TIP:

To make a Reynolds Do-It-Yourself (DIY) Grill Pan, stack two sheets of Reynolds Wrap Heavy Duty Aluminum Foil. Flip a 13×9×2-inch pan upside down. Press sheets of foil around pan. Remove foil from pan; crimp edges to make a pan. Place DIY Grill Pan on a tray to transport to and from the grill.

Sesame Ginger Scallops

Prep Time: 14 minutes ■ Grill Time: 8 minutes

- 2 sheets Reynolds Wrap® Release® Non-Stick Foil
- ⅔ cup sesame ginger stir-fry sauce, divided
- 1 pound sea scallops
- 1 cup fresh mushrooms, cut in half
- 1 medium green bell pepper, cubed
- 1½ cups fresh pineapple chunks
- 1 medium onion, cut into eighths
- 4 cups assorted salad greens
- 2 tablespoons toasted sesame seeds

COMBINE ⅓ cup stir-fry sauce, scallops and mushrooms in a bowl. Cover with plastic wrap; refrigerate 10 minutes. Drain well; discard sauce. Combine remaining stir-fry sauce, green pepper, pineapple and onion. Drain well; reserve sauce.

PREHEAT grill to medium-high. Make drainage holes in both sheets of Reynolds Wrap Release Non-Stick Foil with a large grilling fork. Place one sheet Reynolds Wrap Release Non-Stick Foil on grill grate with non-stick (dull) side toward food. Immediately arrange green pepper, pineapple and onion on foil sheet.

GRILL 4 minutes on uncovered grill, turning and basting with reserved sauce.

PLACE second foil sheet on grill grate with non-stick (dull) side toward food. Arrange scallops and mushrooms on top.

GRILL all food 4 to 6 minutes longer on uncovered grill, turning and basting with reserved sauce, until done. Serve over salad greens; top with sesame seeds. Drizzle with additional stir-fry sauce, if desired.

Makes 4 servings

Cajun Sausage & Beans Packets

Prep Time: 10 minutes   ■   Grill Time: 12 minutes

- 4 **sheets (12×18 inches *each*) Reynolds Wrap® Heavy Duty Aluminum Foil**
- 1 **pound smoked turkey sausage, cut into ¼-inch-thick slices**
- 2 **cans (15 ounces *each*) black beans, rinsed and drained**
- 1 **can (14½ ounces) diced tomatoes with garlic and onions**
- 1 **medium green bell pepper, chopped**
- 2 **teaspoons Cajun seasoning**
- ¼ **teaspoon cayenne pepper (optional)**

PREHEAT grill to medium-high **OR** oven to 450°F. Combine sausage, beans, tomatoes, green bell pepper and seasonings.

CENTER one-fourth of bean mixture on *each* sheet of Reynolds Wrap Heavy Duty Aluminum Foil.

BRING up foil sides. Double fold top and ends to seal packet, leaving room for heat circulation inside. Repeat to make four packets.

GRILL 12 to 14 minutes in covered grill **OR BAKE** 18 to 20 minutes on a cookie sheet in oven.

Makes 4 servings

Grilled Fruit & Pound Cake

Prep Time: 15 minutes ■ Grill Time: 4 minutes

Reynolds Wrap® Release® Non-Stick Foil
½ **cup honey**
¼ **cup butter, melted**
½ **teaspoon ground cinnamon**
8 **slices pound cake, ½ inch thick**
4 **fresh peaches, peeled and halved**
4 **fresh pineapple slices, ½ inch thick**
2 **fresh bananas, quartered**
Fresh strawberries, hulled and halved
1 **jar (11.75 ounces) hot fudge ice cream topping, heated**

COMBINE honey, butter and cinnamon; set aside.

PREHEAT grill to medium-high. Place Reynolds Wrap Release Non-Stick Foil sheet on grill grate with non-stick (dull) side toward food.

BRUSH one side of cake slices with honey mixture; arrange brushed-side down, on foil.

GRILL 2 minutes in covered grill. Brush tops with honey mixture; turn. Grill 2 minutes longer or until lightly browned. Remove cake from foil.

BRUSH one side of peaches, pineapple and bananas with honey mixture; arrange brushed-side down on foil. Grill 4 minutes in covered grill. Brush tops with honey mixture; turn. Grill 3 to 4 minutes longer or until lightly browned.

REMOVE fruit from foil. Garnish with strawberries; drizzle with hot fudge topping before serving.

REYNOLDS KITCHENS TIP:

To heat the hot fudge topping on the grill, make a foil pan by stacking two twelve-inch-square sheets Reynolds Wrap Release Non-Stick Foil with non-stick (dull) side toward food. Place bowl or round container in center. Shape foil around bowl to form a pan. Crimp foil edges tightly. Remove bowl. Add fudge topping; grill over medium heat, stirring occasionally until hot.

Makes 8 servings

Grilled Cheesy Chicken Nachos

Prep Time: 8 minutes ■ Grill Time: 5 minutes

Reynolds Wrap® Release® Non-Stick Foil
- 4 **cups (about 4 ounces) tortilla chips**
- 2 **cups Mexican style shredded cheese, divided**
- 1 **cup shredded cooked chicken**
- 1 **cup salsa**
- 1 **small tomato, chopped**
- ½ **cup sliced black olives**
- 2 **green onions, sliced**

PREHEAT grill to medium-high indirect heat. For indirect heat, the heat source (coals or gas burner) is on one side of grill. Make a Reynolds Do-It-Yourself (DIY) Grill Pan; place on a tray.

ARRANGE tortilla chips in an even layer in DIY Grill Pan. Sprinkle 1¾ cup cheese over tortilla chips.

COMBINE chicken and salsa; spoon over chips and cheese. Top with tomato, black olives and green onions. Sprinkle with remaining ¼ cup cheese. Slide pan onto grill grate.

GRILL 5 to 7 minutes or until cheese melts over indirect heat (the side of grill with no coals or flame underneath).

REYNOLDS KITCHENS TIP:

To make a Reynolds Do-It-Yourself (DIY) Grill Pan, stack two sheets of Reynolds Wrap Release Non-Stick Foil with non-stick (dull) side facing up. Flip a 13×9×2-inch pan upside down. Press sheets of foil around pan with non-stick (dull) side down. Remove foil from pan; crimp edges to make a pan. Place DIY Grill Pan on a tray to transport to and from the grill.

Makes 6 to 8 servings

Grilled Zucchini with Dill & Feta

Prep Time: 5 minutes ■ Grill Time: 5 minutes

2 **sheets (18×20 inches *each*) Reynolds Wrap® Release® Non-Stick Foil**
4 **zucchini, cut into ½-inch-diagonal slices**
1 **tablespoon olive oil**
1 **teaspoon dill weed**
   Salt and black pepper to taste
½ **cup crumbled feta cheese**

PREHEAT grill to medium-high. Make a Reynolds Do-It-Yourself (DIY) Grill Pan; place on a tray.

TOSS zucchini slices, olive oil, dill weed, salt and pepper. Spread zucchini evenly in DIY Grill pan. Slide foil pan onto grill grate.

GRILL 5 minutes in covered grill until tender and browned, stirring once to ensure even cooking. Slide foil pan from grill onto tray. Sprinkle with feta cheese.

Makes 4 servings

REYNOLDS KITCHENS TIP:

To make a Reynolds Do-It-Yourself (DIY) Grill Pan, stack two sheets of Reynolds Wrap Release Non-Stick Foil with non-stick (dull) side facing up. Flip a 13×9×2-inch pan upside down. Press sheets of foil around pan with non-stick (dull) side down. Remove foil from pan; crimp edges to make a pan. Place DIY Grill Pan on a tray to transport to and from the grill.

North Carolina Barbecue Pork

Prep Time: 15 minutes ■ Grill Time: 1½ hours

1 sheet (18×24 inches) Reynolds Wrap® Heavy Duty Aluminum Foil
3 pounds boneless pork loin or shoulder roast

SEASONING RUB:
- **1 tablespoon sugar**
- **1½ teaspoons salt**
- **1½ teaspoons paprika**
- **½ teaspoon black pepper**

VINEGAR-PEPPER SAUCE:
- **1½ cups cider vinegar**
- **2 tablespoons sugar**
- **1 tablespoon crushed red pepper flakes**
- **1½ teaspoons salt**
- **¼ teaspoon cayenne pepper**
- **1½ teaspoons Worcestershire sauce**
  Hamburger or sandwich buns
  Cole slaw (optional)

PREHEAT grill to medium. Combine all **SEASONING RUB** ingredients. Sprinkle and rub seasoning over roast, turning to coat evenly. Center roast on sheet of Reynolds Wrap Heavy Duty Aluminum Foil. Combine all **VINEGAR-PEPPER SAUCE** ingredients in a measuring cup; set aside.

BRING up foil sides. Double fold one end to seal. Through open end, add ½ cup **VINEGAR-PEPPER SAUCE**; reserve remaining sauce. Double fold remaining end, leaving room for heat circulation inside packet.

GRILL 1½ hours or until roast is tender on medium in covered grill. Carefully remove steamed roast from foil and place directly on grill. Reserve ½ cup **VINEGAR-PEPPER SAUCE** to use on sandwiches. Brush roast generously with remaining **VINEGAR-PEPPER SAUCE**.

CONTINUE grilling 15 to 20 minutes on medium in uncovered grill, brushing with sauce and turning every 5 minutes to cook evenly. Remove roast from grill. Slice and shred roast while warm. Combine with reserved sauce. Serve shredded pork on hamburger buns. Top with cole slaw, if desired.

Makes 10 servings

Packet Potatoes

Prep Time: 10 minutes ■ **Grill Time:** 15 minutes

- 1 **sheet Reynolds Wrap® Release® Non-Stick Foil**
- 1 **small onion, thinly sliced**
- 1⅓ **pounds (4 medium) red potatoes, cut into bite-size pieces**
- 2 **tablespoons olive oil or vegetable oil**
- 1 **teaspoon seasoned salt**
- ½ **teaspoon dried dill weed (optional)**
- ¼ **teaspoon black pepper**

PREHEAT grill to medium-high **OR** oven to 450°F.

CENTER onion on sheet of Reynolds Wrap Release Non-Stick Foil with non-stick (dull) side toward food. Layer potatoes evenly on top of onion. Drizzle with oil. Sprinkle with spices.

BRING up foil sides. Double fold top and ends to seal making one large foil packet, leaving room for heat circulation inside.

GRILL 15 to 20 minutes in covered grill **OR BAKE** 30 to 35 minutes on a cookie sheet in oven.

Makes 4 servings

Rosemary & Garlic Grilled Potatoes

Prep Time: 5 minutes   ■   Grill Time: 20 minutes

Reynolds Wrap® Release® Non-Stick Foil
4 **to 6 garlic cloves, minced**
3 **tablespoons olive oil**
2 **teaspoons dried rosemary**
1 **teaspoon seasoned salt**
½ **teaspoon coarsely ground black pepper**
4 **large red potatoes, cut into 1 inch cubes**

PREHEAT grill to medium-high.

MAKE a Reynolds Do-It-Yourself (DIY) Grill Pan; place on a tray.

COMBINE all ingredients in a large bowl; toss to coat potatoes. Spread potatoes evenly in DIY Grill Pan. Slide foil pan onto grill grate.

GRILL 20 to 25 minutes in covered grill or until potatoes are tender and crispy, turning once. Slide foil pan from grill onto tray.

Makes 4 servings

REYNOLDS KITCHENS TIP:

To make a Reynolds Do-It-Yourself (DIY) Grill Pan, stack two sheets of Reynolds Wrap Release Non-Stick Foil with non-stick (dull) side facing up. Flip a 13×9×2-inch pan upside down. Press sheets of foil around pan with non-stick (dull) side down. Remove foil from pan; crimp edges to make a pan. Place DIY Grill Pan on a tray to transport to and from the grill.

Grilled Corn-on-the-Cob

Prep Time: 5 minutes ■ Grill Time: 15 minutes

1   sheet (18×24 inches) Reynolds Wrap® Heavy Duty Aluminum Foil
4   ears corn-on-the-cob, husked
¼   cup butter OR margarine, softened
    Seasoned salt
    Black pepper
2   ice cubes

PREHEAT grill to medium-high **OR** oven to 450°F.

CENTER corn on sheet of Reynolds Wrap Heavy Duty Aluminum Foil. Spread butter on corn. Sprinkle with seasonings. Top with ice cubes.

BRING up foil sides. Double fold top and ends to seal making one large foil packet, leaving room for heat circulation inside.

GRILL 15 to 20 minutes in covered grill, turning packet over once **OR BAKE** 35 to 40 minutes on a cookie sheet in oven.

Makes 4 servings

REYNOLDS KITCHENS TIP:

Substitute olive oil for the butter, if desired.

Broccoli & Cauliflower Parmesan Packet

Prep Time: 10 minutes ■ **Grill Time:** 12 minutes

- 1 **sheet Reynolds Wrap® Heavy Duty Aluminum Foil**
- 4 **cups broccoli florets**
- 2½ **cups cauliflower florets**
- ½ **cup sun-dried tomatoes**
- 3 **tablespoons olive oil**
- 2 **cloves garlic, minced**
- 1 **teaspoon dried basil**
- ⅓ **cup grated Parmesan cheese**
- 4 **ice cubes**

PREHEAT grill to medium-high **OR** oven to 450°F. Combine broccoli, cauliflower, sun-dried tomatoes, olive oil, garlic and basil in a large bowl.

CENTER vegetable mixture on sheet of Reynolds Wrap Heavy Duty Aluminum Foil. Sprinkle with Parmesan cheese; top with ice cubes.

BRING up foil sides. Double fold top and ends to seal making one large packet, leaving room for heat circulation inside.

GRILL 12 to 15 minutes in covered grill **OR BAKE** 20 to 25 minutes on a cookie sheet in oven.

Makes 6 servings

Southwestern Pork Quesadillas

Prep Time: 18 minutes ■ Grill Time: 14 minutes

- 2 sheets Reynolds Wrap® Release® Non-Stick Foil
- 1 pound pork tenderloin, sliced ½ inch thick
- ½ package (1.25 ounces) Southwestern-style marinade
- 3 tablespoons vegetable oil, divided
- 1 tablespoon water
- 1 tablespoon white vinegar
- 4 flour tortillas (9 to 10 inches *each*)
- ½ cup black bean dip
- 1 cup shredded Monterey Jack cheese
- ½ cup chunky salsa
- 1 medium red onion, cut into ¼-inch-thick slices
-    Salsa and sour cream

COMBINE pork, marinade, two tablespoons oil, water and vinegar; set aside. Brush one side of tortillas with remaining vegetable oil. With oiled side down, layer bean dip, cheese and salsa on half of each tortilla; set aside.

PREHEAT grill to medium-high. Drain pork well; discard marinade. Brush onion with oil. Make drainage holes in both sheets of Reynolds Wrap Release Non-Stick Foil with a large grilling fork. Place one foil sheet on grill grate with non-stick (dull) side toward food. Immediately arrange pork and onion on foil sheet.

GRILL 10 to 12 minutes on uncovered grill, turning once, until done. Remove food from foil sheet. Arrange pork and onion on top of salsa on tortilla; fold tortilla over filling.

PLACE second foil sheet on grill rack with non-stick (dull) side toward food. Arrange folded tortillas on top. Grill 4 to 5 minutes on uncovered grill, turning once, until browned. Remove quesadillas from foil sheet. Cut into wedges; serve with salsa and sour cream.

Makes 4 servings

Grilled Salsa Marinated Sirloin

Prep Time: 5 minutes ■ Grill Time: 16 minutes

Reynolds® Plastic Wrap
- 1 **cup chunky salsa**
- ¼ **cup fresh lime juice**
- ¼ **cup water**
- 2 **tablespoons vegetable or olive oil**
- 1 **teaspoon ground cumin**
- 1 **(1½- to 1¾-pound) boneless beef sirloin steak, cut 1¼ to 1½ inches thick**

COMBINE salsa, lime juice, water, oil and cumin in a shallow glass baking dish. Add steak, turning to coat with marinade.

COVER with Reynolds Plastic Wrap. Marinate in refrigerator 6 hours or overnight. Remove steak from marinade; drain. Discard marinade.

PREHEAT grill to medium-high.

GRILL steak 8 to 10 minutes on *each* side for medium-rare. Slice steak into ½-inch-thick strips.

Makes 4 servings

Grill Roasted Corn & Black Bean Salsa

Prep Time: 15 minutes ■ Grill Time: 15 minutes ■ Chill Time: 30 minutes

Reynolds Wrap® Release® Non-Stick Foil
- 2 **ears fresh corn-on-the-cob**
- 1 **tablespoon garlic-flavored olive oil**
- 1 **can (15.5 ounces) black beans, rinsed and drained**
- 1 **small red bell pepper, diced**
- 1 **small jalapeño pepper, seeded and chopped**
- ⅓ **cup chopped red onion**
- ¼ **cup chopped fresh cilantro**
- 3 **tablespoons fresh lime juice**
- ½ **teaspoon salt**
- ½ **teaspoon ground cumin**

PREHEAT grill to medium-high. Make drainage holes in two sheets of Reynolds Wrap Release Non-Stick Foil with a large grilling fork; set aside.

BRUSH corn with garlic-flavored olive oil; set aside.

PLACE a sheet of foil with holes on grill rack with non-stick (dull) side toward food; immediately place corn on foil. Grill 15 to 20 minutes; turning occasionally until corn is brown and roasted. Remove corn from foil; discard foil.

CUT corn from cob; combine with remaining ingredients in a medium bowl. Cover with Reynolds Plastic Wrap; refrigerate 30 minutes.

Makes 4 servings

Greek Chicken Packets

Antipasto Appetizer Squares

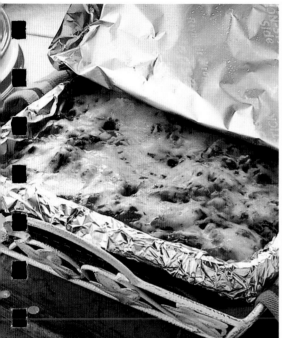

Layered Tortilla Casserole

Ginger Shrimp & Broccoli en Papillote

Easy Cleanup Meals

Ginger Shrimp & Broccoli en Papillote

Prep Time: 15 minutes ■ Cook Time: 13 minutes

Reynolds® Parchment Paper
4 **cups broccoli florets**
2 **cloves garlic, minced**
1 **tablespoon sesame oil**
½ **tablespoon grated fresh ginger**
½ **tablespoon soy sauce**
1 **pound shrimp, peeled and deveined**

PREHEAT oven to 400°F. Tear off four fifteen-inch sheets of Reynolds Parchment Paper. Fold each sheet in half and crease it in the center. Unfold.

DIVIDE broccoli evenly on one-half of *each* sheet near crease.

MIX garlic, sesame oil, ginger and soy sauce until well blended. Add shrimp; stir to coat evenly. Divide shrimp evenly among packets.

FOLD over other half of *each* sheet to enclose ingredients. Starting at top corner, make small overlapping folds down entire length of packet to seal edges together. Twist the last fold several times to make a tight seal. Repeat to make four packets. Place parchment packets on a large cookie sheet.

BAKE 13 to 15 minutes. Place parchment packets on dinner plates. Carefully cut an "✕" in the top of *each* packet to allow steam to escape. Serve immediately.

Makes 4 servings

Caribbean Jerk Chicken Packets

Prep Time: 10 minutes ■ Cook Time: 20 minutes

- 4 **sheets (12×18 inches *each*) Reynolds Wrap® Heavy Duty Aluminum Foil**
- 2 **cups cooked rice**
- 1 **can (16 ounces) red beans OR light red kidney beans, rinsed and drained**
- ½ **cup Caribbean jerk marinade, divided**
- 4 **skinless, boneless chicken breast halves (1 to 1¼ pounds)**

PREHEAT oven to 450°F **OR** grill to medium-high. Combine rice, beans and ¼-cup marinade.

CENTER one-fourth of mixture on *each* sheet of Reynolds Wrap Heavy Duty Aluminum Foil. Top with chicken; drizzle with remaining marinade.

BRING up foil sides. Double fold top and ends to seal packet, leaving room for heat circulation inside. Repeat to make four packets.

BAKE 20 to 24 minutes on a cookie sheet in oven **OR GRILL** 16 to 20 minutes in covered grill.

Makes 4 servings

Hawaiian Fish Packets

Prep Time: 10 minutes   ■   Cook Time: 12 minutes

- **4 sheets (12×18 inches *each*) Reynolds Wrap® Release® Non-Stick Foil**
- **4 fish fillets (4 to 6 ounces *each*)**
- **1 can (15¼ ounces) pineapple chunks, drained (reserve juice)**
- **1 medium green bell pepper, cut into strips**
- **3 tablespoons teriyaki sauce**
- **1 tablespoon packed brown sugar**
- **¼ teaspoon ground ginger**

PREHEAT oven to 450°F **OR** grill to medium-high.

CENTER one fish fillet on *each* sheet of Reynolds Wrap Release Non-Stick Foil with non-stick (dull) side toward food. Top with pineapple and green pepper. Combine one tablespoon reserved pineapple juice, teriyaki sauce, brown sugar and ginger. Spoon one-fourth of mixture over fish, pineapple and peppers.

BRING up foil sides. Double fold top and ends to seal packet, leaving room for heat circulation inside. Repeat to make four packets.

BAKE 12 to 14 minutes on a cookie sheet in oven **OR GRILL** 8 to 10 minutes in covered grill.

Makes 4 servings

Orange Teriyaki Beef Roast

Prep Time: 15 minutes ■ Cook Time: 35 minutes

- 1 Reynolds® Oven Bag, Large Size
- 2 tablespoons all-purpose flour
- ½ cup orange juice
- ½ cup teriyaki sauce
- ¼ cup packed brown sugar
- 3 cloves garlic, minced
- 1 teaspoon grated orange peel
- ½ teaspoon crushed red pepper flakes
- 1 (2-pound) beef top round roast, 1-inch thick
  Hot cooked rice (optional)
- ¼ cup sliced green onions

SHAKE flour in Reynolds Oven Bag; place in 13×9×2-inch or larger baking pan at least two inches deep.

ADD orange juice, teriyaki sauce, brown sugar, garlic, orange peel and crushed red pepper to oven bag. Squeeze bag to blend in flour. Add beef to bag. Turn bag to coat beef with sauce.

CLOSE oven bag with nylon tie. Marinate beef in refrigerator 1½ to 2 hours.

PREHEAT oven to 325°F. Cut six ½-inch slits in top of oven bag. Tuck ends of bag in pan.

BAKE 35 to 45 minutes or until meat thermometer reads 145°F (do not overcook). Thinly slice beef. Stir sauce; serve with rice, if desired. Sprinkle with sliced green onions.

Makes 8 (3-ounce) servings

Antipasto Appetizer Squares

Prep Time: 15 minutes ■ Cook Time: 18 minutes

Reynolds® Parchment Paper
1 **package (13.8 ounces) refrigerated pizza crust**
1 **jar (6 ounces) marinated artichoke hearts, drained, coarsely chopped**
1 **cup chopped tomatoes**
1 **cup thinly sliced deli salami**
1 **cup shredded Italian-style blended cheese**
2 **tablespoons chopped fresh basil**
½ **teaspoon dried Italian seasoning**
¼ **teaspoon garlic powder**

PREHEAT oven to 425°F. Line 15×11-inch baking pan with Reynolds Parchment Paper.

UNROLL pizza crust on parchment paper. Press to form 14×10-inch rectangle. Generously prick dough with fork.

BAKE 11 minutes or until golden brown. Remove from oven.

SPREAD artichoke hearts, tomatoes, salami, cheese and basil evenly over crust. Sprinkle with Italian seasoning and garlic powder.

BAKE an additional 7 to 10 minutes or until cheese is melted. Cut into squares and serve warm.

REYNOLDS KITCHENS TIP

For crispier crust, prebake crust an additional 2 to 3 minutes before adding toppings.

Makes 32 servings

Pecan Coconut Crusted Fish

Prep Time: 20 minutes ■ Cook Time: 15 minutes

Reynolds Wrap® Release® Non-Stick Foil

PECAN COATING:

¼ **cup butter, melted**
½ **teaspoon salt**
¼ **to ½ teaspoon cayenne pepper**
4 **fish fillets (4 to 6 ounce) fresh or thawed**
½ **cup finely chopped pecans**
½ **cup shredded coconut**
2 **tablespoons plain dry bread crumbs**

PINEAPPLE-MANGO SALSA:

2 **cans (8 ounces *each*) pineapple tidbits, drained**
1 **large mango, diced**
½ **of a medium red bell pepper, diced**
2 **green onions, chopped**
1 **tablespoon red wine vinegar**
2 **tablespoons chopped fresh cilantro**
¼ **teaspoon salt**

PREHEAT oven to 400°F. Line a 15×10×1-inch baking pan with Reynolds Wrap Release Non-Stick Foil with non-stick (dull) side toward food; set aside.

COMBINE butter, salt and cayenne pepper in a large bowl. Add fish and stir to coat; set aside. Combine pecans, coconut and bread crumbs on a sheet of wax paper. Roll fish in coconut mixture, turning to coat evenly. Press on additional mixture, if necessary. Place in a single layer in foil-lined pan.

BAKE 15 to 20 minutes or until fish is opaque throughout.

TO MAKE PINEAPPLE-MANGO SALSA, combine pineapple, mango, red pepper, green onions, red wine vinegar, cilantro and salt. Chill; serve with fish.

Makes 4 servings

Layered Tortilla Casserole

Prep Time: 15 minutes　■　Cook Time: 45 minutes

Reynolds Wrap® Release® Non-Stick Foil
12　**corn tortillas (4 inches), lightly toasted**
3　**cups coarsely chopped cooked chicken**
1　**package (10 ounces) frozen cut-leaf spinach, thawed and
　　well drained**
　　Salt and black pepper to taste
5　**cups tomato sauce**
1　**package (8 ounces) shredded Mexican cheese blend, divided**
1　**can (15¼ ounces) whole kernel corn, drained**
2　**poblano chiles, roasted and cut into strips**

PREHEAT oven to 350°F. Line a 13×9×2-inch baking pan with Reynolds Wrap Release Non-Stick Foil with non-stick (dull) side toward food; set aside.

CUT tortillas in half. Arrange about twelve tortilla halves to cover as much of the bottom of pan as possible. Top with chicken and spinach; sprinkle with salt and pepper. Spoon half of sauce and half of cheese over spinach. Arrange remaining tortilla halves over cheese. Top with corn, chiles, remaining sauce and cheese.

COVER with a sheet of non-stick foil with dull side toward food.

BAKE 30 minutes. **UNCOVER and BAKE** 15 to 20 minutes longer or until cheese is melted. Let stand 5 to 10 minutes before cutting into squares to serve.

Makes 8 to 10 servings

REYNOLDS KITCHENS TIP

To make a quick tomato sauce, combine 1 jar (16 ounces) chunky salsa, 2 cups water, 1 can (6 ounces) tomato paste, 2 tablespoons chopped chipotle chilies in adobo sauce, 2 cloves minced garlic and 2 tablespoons chopped fresh cilantro.

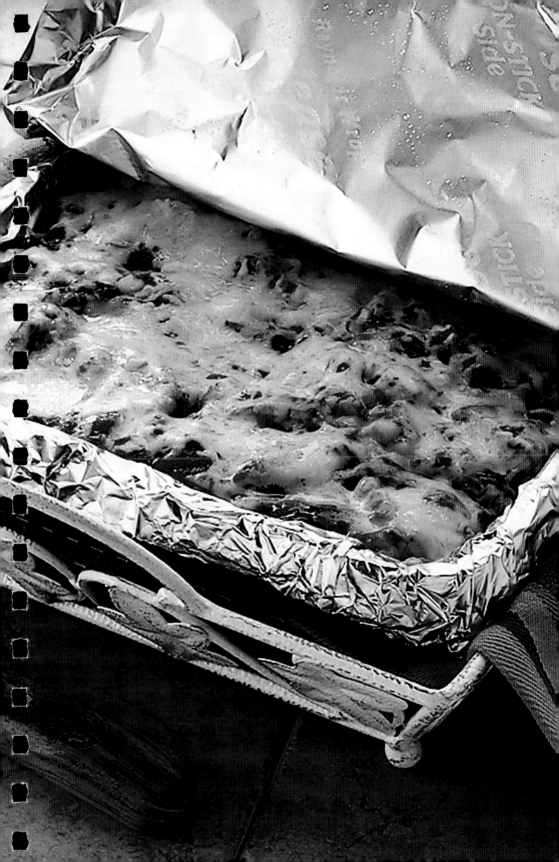

Satay-Style Beef

Prep Time: 10 minutes ■ Cook Time: 14 minutes

- 4 **sheets (12×18 inches *each*) Reynolds Wrap® Heavy Duty Aluminum Foil**
- 1 **pound beef top sirloin steak, ½ inch thick, fat trimmed**
- 3 **cups fresh snow peas**
- ⅓ **cup reduced-sodium teriyaki sauce**
- 2½ **tablespoons creamy peanut butter**
- ¾ **teaspoon cornstarch**
- 1 **package (8 ounces) angel hair pasta, cooked and drained**
- 2 **plum tomatoes, chopped**
- 4 **green onions, sliced**

PREHEAT oven to 450°F **OR** grill to medium-high. Slice steak across the grain into thin strips.

CENTER one-fourth of beef strips on *each* sheet of Reynolds Wrap Heavy Duty Aluminum Foil. Top with snow peas. Combine teriyaki sauce, peanut butter and cornstarch; mix until smooth and well blended. Pour one-fourth of teriyaki mixture evenly over meat and vegetables.

BRING up foil sides. Double fold top and ends to seal packet, leaving room for heat circulation inside. Repeat to make four packets.

BAKE 14 to 18 minutes on a cookie sheet in oven **OR GRILL** 10 to 14 minutes in covered grill. Serve over angel hair pasta. Sprinkle *each* serving with tomatoes and green onions.

Makes 4 servings

Greek Chicken Packets

Prep Time: 10 minutes ■ Cook Time: 23 minutes

Reynolds Wrap® Release® Non-Stick Foil
2   **boneless, skinless chicken breast halves (½ to ¾ pounds)**
4   **ounces uncooked angel hair pasta**
1   **tablespoon olive oil**
¼   **cup julienne-cut sun-dried tomatoes**
1   **jar (6 ounces) marinated artichoke hearts, drained**
½   **cup feta cheese with garlic and herbs, crumbled**
8   **ice cubes**
1   **cup water**

PREHEAT oven to 450°F **OR** grill to medium-high.

CENTER one chicken breast half on *each* sheet of Reynolds Wrap Release Non-Stick Foil with non-stick (dull) side toward food. Break angel hair pasta in half and place beside chicken. Drizzle olive oil over pasta. Arrange tomatoes and artichoke hearts over chicken. Top with feta cheese. Place ice cubes over pasta.

BRING up foil sides. Double fold top and one end. Through open end, pour in ½ cup water. Double fold remaining end to seal packet, leaving room for heat circulation inside. Repeat to make two packets.

BAKE 23 to 25 minutes on a cookie sheet in oven **OR GRILL** 12 to 14 minutes in covered grill. Fluff pasta with a fork before serving.

REYNOLDS KITCHENS TIP

To pour liquids into packets, hold packets at a slight angle. After folding ends to seal, turn folded ends up to prevent leaking.

Makes 2 servings

Far East Spiced Chicken Packets

Prep Time: 10 minutes ■ Cook Time: 18 minutes

- 2 **sheets (12×18 inches *each*) Reynolds Wrap® Release® Non-Stick Foil**
- 1 **teaspoon ground cinnamon**
- ½ **teaspoon ground coriander**
- ¼ **teaspoon ground cumin**
- 2 **boneless, skinless chicken breast halves (½ pound)**
- 1 **medium red bell pepper, cut into strips**
- 4 **green onions, cut into 1-inch pieces**
- ¼ **cup apricot preserves OR orange marmalade**
- 2 **tablespoons orange juice**
  Garlic salt to taste
  Apricot Rice Pilaf (recipe follows)

PREHEAT oven to 450°F **OR** grill to medium-high.

COMBINE spices. Sprinkle and rub spices over chicken, turning to coat evenly. Center one chicken breast half on *each* sheet of Reynolds Wrap Release Non-Stick Foil with non-stick (dull) side toward food. Top with red pepper strips and green onions. Drizzle with apricot preserves and orange juice. Sprinkle with garlic salt.

BRING up foil sides. Double fold top and ends to seal packet, leaving room for heat circulation inside. Repeat to make two packets.

BAKE 18 to 22 minutes on cookie sheet in oven **OR GRILL** 14 to 18 minutes in covered grill. Serve over Apricot Rice Pilaf.

Makes 2 servings

Apricot Rice Pilaf

- 10 **dried apricots, chopped**
- 1 **cup rice, uncooked**

STIR apricots into uncooked rice; cook following package directions.

Bahamian Snapper Packets

Prep Time: 15 minutes   ■   Cook Time: 10 minutes

- **4 sheets (12×18 inches *each*) Reynolds Wrap® Release® Non-Stick Foil**
- **4 red snapper fillets (4 to 6 ounces *each*)**
- **½ fresh mango, diced**
- **½ fresh papaya, diced**
- **½ small onion, chopped**
- **2 tablespoons fresh lime juice**
- **2 tablespoons grated fresh ginger**
- **½ small jalapeno pepper, seeded and finely chopped**
- **1 teaspoon salt**
- **½ teaspoon chopped fresh thyme**
- **½ teaspoon chopped fresh parsley**
- **½ teaspoon whole cloves**
- **Black pepper to taste**

PREHEAT oven to 450°F **OR** preheat grill to medium-high.

CENTER one fish fillet on *each* sheet of Reynolds Wrap Release Non-Stick Foil with non-stick (dull) side toward food. Combine remaining ingredients; spoon one-fourth of mixture over fish.

BRING up foil sides. Double fold top and ends to seal packet, leaving room for heat circulation inside. Repeat to make four packets.

BAKE 15 to 18 minutes on a cookie sheet in oven **OR GRILL** 8 to 10 minutes in covered grill.

Makes 4 servings

Thai Peanut Chicken and Vegetables

Prep Time: 14 minutes   ■   Grill Time: 7 minutes

- 2 **sheets Reynolds Wrap® Release® Non-Stick Foil**
- 1 **pound boneless, skinless chicken breast tenders**
- ¼ **cup Thai peanut sauce**
- 1½ **cups snow peas**
- 1 **cup peeled baby carrots, cut in half lengthwise**
- 1 **medium red bell pepper, cut into strips**
- 1 **medium onion, cut into eighths**
- 1 **tablespoon vegetable oil**
- 1 **teaspoon garlic salt**
-   **Hot cooked rice**
- ⅓ **cup chopped peanuts**

PREHEAT grill to medium-high.

COMBINE chicken tenders and Thai peanut sauce in a bowl; set aside. Combine vegetables, oil and garlic salt in another bowl. Make drainage holes in sheets of Reynolds Wrap Release Non-Stick Foil with a large grilling fork.

PLACE foil sheets on grill grate with non-stick (dull) side toward food. Immediately arrange chicken on one foil sheet. Arrange vegetables evenly on second foil sheet.

GRILL 7 to 8 minutes on uncovered grill, turning chicken once and turning vegetables frequently, until chicken is done and vegetables are crisp-tender.

REMOVE chicken and vegetables from foil sheets. Serve over rice topped with chopped peanuts and additional Thai peanut sauce.

Makes 4 Servings

REYNOLDS KITCHENS TIP

To make your own Thai peanut sauce, combine ⅔ cup thick teriyaki sauce, ¼ cup creamy peanut butter and ¼ teaspoon crushed red pepper flakes.

Moroccan-Style Chicken & Vegetable Packets

Prep Time: 8 minutes ■ Cook Time: 20 minutes

- 2 sheets (12×18 inches *each*) Reynolds Wrap® Release® Non-Stick Foil
- 2 boneless, skinless chicken breast halves (4 to 6 ounces *each*)
- 1½ teaspoons ground cumin
- ½ teaspoon ground cinnamon
- ½ teaspoon salt
- ½ teaspoon black pepper
- 1 can (14½ ounces) diced tomatoes, drained
- 1 medium zucchini, sliced into 2-inch strips

PREHEAT oven to 450°F **OR** grill to medium-high.

CENTER one chicken breast half on *each* sheet of Reynolds Wrap Release Non-Stick Foil with non-stick (dull) side toward food. Combine cumin, cinnamon, salt and pepper; sprinkle ½ teaspoon mixture over chicken. Combine tomatoes with remaining spice mixture; spoon over chicken. Arrange zucchini strips over chicken and tomatoes.

BRING up foil sides. Double fold top and ends to seal packet, leaving room for heat circulation inside. Repeat to make two packets.

BAKE 20 to 22 minutes on a cookie sheet in oven **OR GRILL** 10 to 12 minutes in covered grill.

Makes 2 servings

REYNOLDS KITCHENS TIP

Sprinkle with chopped fresh cilantro, if desired. Serve with hot cooked couscous or rice.

Mexican Bread Dessert

Prep Time: 30 minutes ■ Cook Time: 25 minutes

Reynolds Wrap® Release® Non-Stick Foil
1 **pound white bread, cut into 1-inch pieces**
3 **cups (1 pound) packed dark brown sugar**
2 **cups water**
2 **cups apple juice**
¼ **cup (½ stick) butter**
1 **cinnamon stick**
4 **whole cloves**
1 **cup pecan pieces, toasted**
1 **cup raisins**
2 **cups (5 ounces) grated queso fresco or Monterey Jack cheese**

PREHEAT oven to 350°F.

LINE a 15½×10½×1-inch pan with Reynolds Wrap Release Non-Stick Foil with non-stick (dull) side toward food. Spread bread cubes in a single layer in foil-lined pan. Turning the bread cubes once or twice, bake about 15 minutes to dry the bread without browning.

COMBINE brown sugar, water, apple juice, butter, cinnamon and cloves in a large saucepan. Bring to a boil; reduce heat and simmer, stirring occasionally, until the mixture is a light syrup, 15 to 20 minutes.

LINE a 13×9×2-inch baking pan with non-stick foil with non-stick (dull) side toward food.

COMBINE bread cubes, pecans and raisins in a large bowl. Strain syrup into the bowl; stir to mix. Let stand a few minutes for bread to absorb syrup. Stir in cheese. Spread mixture in an even layer in foil-lined pan.

BAKE 25 to 30 minutes or until top is crisp.

Makes 8 to 10 servings

Curried Chicken with Rice & Peas Packets

Prep Time: 13 minutes   ■   Cook Time: 20 minutes

- 2 **sheets (12×18 inches** *each***) Reynolds Wrap® Release® Non-Stick Foil**
- 2 **boneless, skinless chicken breast halves (4 to 6 ounces** *each***)**
- 1½ **teaspoons curry powder, divided**
- 1 **cup instant white or brown rice**
- 1 **cup frozen peas and carrots**
- ¼ **cup raisins**
- 1 **cup chicken broth, divided**

PREHEAT oven to 450°F **OR** grill to medium-high.

CENTER one chicken breast half on *each* sheet of Reynolds Wrap Release Non-Stick Foil with non-stick (dull) side toward food. Coat *each* chicken breast half with ¼ teaspoon curry powder. Combine rice, peas and carrots, raisins, ½ cup chicken broth and remaining curry powder; spoon mixture around chicken.

BRING up foil sides. Double fold top and one end. Through open end, pour ¼ cup remaining chicken broth. Double fold remaining end to seal packet, leaving room for heat circulation inside. Repeat to make two packets.

BAKE 20 to 25 minutes on a cookie sheet in oven **OR GRILL** 12 to 14 minutes in covered grill.

Makes 2 servings

REYNOLDS KITCHENS TIP

Serve with prepared mango chutney, if desired.

Baked Chiles Rellenos with Roasted Corn

Prep Time: **30** minutes   ■   Cook Time: **35** minutes

Reynolds Wrap® Release® Non-Stick Foil
- 8 **poblano chiles**
- 1 **can (15¼ ounces) whole kernel corn, drained**
- 2 **tablespoons vegetable oil**
- ½ **cup chopped roasted red pepper**
- ½ **cup chopped cilantro**
  Salt and black pepper
- 2 **cups grated Monterey Jack cheese**
- 1 **cup cornmeal**
- ½ **cup dry bread crumbs**
- 3 **tablespoons vegetable oil**
- 3 **eggs, lightly beaten**

ROAST chiles under broiler, on the grill or over a flame until charred. Wrap in Reynolds Plastic Wrap and let "sweat" about 10 minutes to loosen skin; peel. Carefully slit each chile down the side from just under the stem area to one-half-inch above the bottom pointed end. Scoop out all seeds; set aside.

PREHEAT oven to 450°F. Line a 15×10×1-inch pan with Reynolds Wrap Release Non-Stick Foil with non-stick (dull) side toward food. Combine corn and vegetable oil. Spread in an even layer in foil-lined pan.

BAKE 20 to 25 minutes, stirring frequently until corn is roasted; let cool. Set pan aside.

COMBINE roasted corn, red pepper, cilantro, salt and pepper. Stir in cheese. Stuff mixture into poblano chiles, overlapping the sides to enclose mixture.

MIX cornmeal, bread crumbs and oil in a shallow bowl with a fork until well blended. Place eggs in another shallow bowl. Dip stuffed peppers into eggs, then into cornmeal mixture. Place on a foil-lined pan.

BAKE 15 to 20 minutes or until golden brown. Serve with your favorite tomato sauce or salsa.

Makes 8 servings

METRIC CONVERSION CHART

VOLUME MEASUREMENTS (dry)

1/8 teaspoon = 0.5 mL
1/4 teaspoon = 1 mL
1/2 teaspoon = 2 mL
3/4 teaspoon = 4 mL
1 teaspoon = 5 mL
1 tablespoon = 15 mL
2 tablespoons = 30 mL
1/4 cup = 60 mL
1/3 cup = 75 mL
1/2 cup = 125 mL
2/3 cup = 150 mL
3/4 cup = 175 mL
1 cup = 250 mL
2 cups = 1 pint = 500 mL
3 cups = 750 mL
4 cups = 1 quart = 1 L

VOLUME MEASUREMENTS (fluid)

1 fluid ounce (2 tablespoons) = 30 mL
4 fluid ounces (1/2 cup) = 125 mL
8 fluid ounces (1 cup) = 250 mL
12 fluid ounces (1 1/2 cups) = 375 mL
16 fluid ounces (2 cups) = 500 mL

WEIGHTS (mass)

1/2 ounce = 15 g
1 ounce = 30 g
3 ounces = 90 g
4 ounces = 120 g
8 ounces = 225 g
10 ounces = 285 g
12 ounces = 360 g
16 ounces = 1 pound = 450 g

DIMENSIONS

1/16 inch = 2 mm
1/8 inch = 3 mm
1/4 inch = 6 mm
1/2 inch = 1.5 cm
3/4 inch = 2 cm
1 inch = 2.5 cm

OVEN TEMPERATURES

250°F = 120°C
275°F = 140°C
300°F = 150°C
325°F = 160°C
350°F = 180°C
375°F = 190°C
400°F = 200°C
425°F = 220°C
450°F = 230°C

BAKING PAN SIZES

Utensil	Size in Inches/Quarts	Metric Volume	Size in Centimeters
Baking or Cake Pan (square or rectangular)	8×8×2	2 L	20×20×5
	9×9×2	2.5 L	23×23×5
	12×8×2	3 L	30×20×5
	13×9×2	3.5 L	33×23×5
Loaf Pan	8×4×3	1.5 L	20×10×7
	9×5×3	2 L	23×13×7
Round Layer Cake Pan	8×1½	1.2 L	20×4
	9×1½	1.5 L	23×4
Pie Plate	8×1¼	750 mL	20×3
	9×1¼	1 L	23×3
Baking Dish or Casserole	1 quart	1 L	—
	1½ quarts	1.5 L	—
	2 quarts	2 L	—